China's
AI Exports

Technology Distribution and Data Safety

JENNIFER BOUEY, LYNN HU, KELLER SCHOLL, WILLIAM
MARCELLINO, RAFIQ DOSSANI, AMMAR A. MALIK, KYRA
SOLOMON, SHENG ZHANG, ANDY SHUFER

A Research Lab at William & Mary

NATIONAL SECURITY RESEARCH DIVISION

For more information on this publication, visit **www.rand.org/t/RRA2696-2**.

About RAND

The RAND Corporation is a research organization that develops solutions to public policy challenges to help make communities throughout the world safer and more secure, healthier and more prosperous. RAND is nonprofit, nonpartisan, and committed to the public interest. To learn more about RAND, visit www.rand.org.

Research Integrity

Our mission to help improve policy and decisionmaking through research and analysis is enabled through our core values of quality and objectivity and our unwavering commitment to the highest level of integrity and ethical behavior. To help ensure our research and analysis are rigorous, objective, and nonpartisan, we subject our research publications to a robust and exacting quality-assurance process; avoid both the appearance and reality of financial and other conflicts of interest through staff training, project screening, and a policy of mandatory disclosure; and pursue transparency in our research engagements through our commitment to the open publication of our research findings and recommendations, disclosure of the source of funding of published research, and policies to ensure intellectual independence. For more information, visit www.rand.org/about/research-integrity.

RAND's publications do not necessarily reflect the opinions of its research clients and sponsors.

Published by the RAND Corporation, Santa Monica, Calif.
© 2023 RAND Corporation
RAND® is a registered trademark.

Library of Congress Cataloging-in-Publication Data is available for this publication.
ISBN:978-1-9774-1240-9

Cover: Cover composite from images by Issaronow/Adobe Stock and Tanarch/Adobe Stock.

About This Report

In recent years, China's aspiration for global technology leadership has driven its significant investments in artificial intelligence (AI) for national security, economic growth, and societal well-being. Although there is increasing research on China's domestic AI development ecosystems and drivers, the details of China's development-financed AI exports remain elusive. Despite being the single-largest provider of foreign development assistance, Beijing does not participate in any aid or debt transparency initiatives.

To address this gap, researchers from the RAND Corporation and AidData jointly built a new database on China's AI export projects that are funded with official development financing: China's AI Exports Database (CAIED). CAIED uses data from multiple public databases and indexes related to Chinese global finance and recipient countries' electoral democracy, freedom, and data protection and privacy status. This report includes the first analysis that uses CAIED. Simultaneously, we also conducted qualitative country case studies to examine the recipient countries' public sentiments about China's AI export. Our specific research questions are as follows:

- How have AI exports financed by the Chinese government changed between 2000 and 2017 (the latest year for which data were available)?
- Which countries, industry sectors, and social domains are the most affected by China's AI exports?
- What factors make China's AI exports competitive in the developing world?
- How does the public in recipient countries perceive China's AI exports?

RAND researchers collaborated with AidData to create a first-of-its-kind interactive tool, showing China's AI influence in the developing world. The publications in this series are the first published studies to use quantitative and qualitative metrics to examine China's AI technology exports. The analysis summarized in this series reflects data available to the research team from AidData's Global Chinese Development Finance (GCDF) Dataset version 2.0, which covers the years 2000–2017. An updated GCDF 3.0 was made available in November 2023, and the research team is working on analyzing the new dataset, which extends the time horizon covered through 2021.

RAND National Security Research Division

The research was funded by RAND-initiated research and conducted within the Acquisition and Technology Policy Center of the RAND National Security Research Division (NSRD), which operates the National Defense Research Institute (NDRI), a federally funded research and development center sponsored by the Office of the Secretary of Defense, the Joint Staff, the Unified Combatant Commands, the Navy, the Marine Corps, the defense agencies, and the defense intelligence enterprise.

Funding

Funding for this research was made possible by the independent research and development provisions of RAND's contracts for the operation of its U.S. Department of Defense federally funded research and development centers.

Acknowledgments

We thank our external partners, including the entire AidData data team, Andy Shufer (AidData), and Mwangi Mwaura (Oxford University), for participating in data collection and analysis. We are also grateful to our external quality assurance reviewer, Anita Plummer from Howard University, and RAND reviewer James Ryseff for their insightful comments.

We would like to thank several individuals within RAND for providing the support and resources necessary to conduct this effort. RAND-Initiated Research Director Lisa Jaycox provided encouragement and thoughtful suggestions throughout the project. We appreciate the NSRD quality assurance team, Saci Haslam, Aaron Frank, and Jim Powers, for their coordination, reviews, comments, and approval. We also thank communications analyst Kristin Leuschner for revising the report and Stacey Yi for project coordination. The report also benefited from the hard work of the RAND publication team; Jaron Feldman and Fadia Afashe were especially helpful for the final format of the report. All errors or omissions remain the sole responsibility of the authors.

Finally, we would like to especially thank Maria Patel for her generous introductions to Pakistan's stakeholders and her expert support throughout the research process. We also thank Eric Brown at William & Mary's Global Research Institute for reviewing earlier drafts.

Summary

In 2021, China unveiled a strategy to position itself as a foremost technological power by 2035, building on the momentum from 2010 when its burgeoning economy and technological advancements spurred aspirations for supercomputing dominance.[1] This ambition has ignited a strong political will in China to invest in artificial intelligence (AI) for national security, economic development, and societal welfare. Although there is increasing research and analysis on China's domestic AI development ecosystems and drivers, the details of China's development-financed AI exports remain elusive. Despite being the single-largest provider of foreign development assistance, Beijing does not participate in aid or debt transparency initiatives.

To address this gap, researchers from the RAND Corporation and AidData jointly built a new database on China's AI export projects that are funded with official development financing: China's AI Exports Database (CAIED). CAIED uses data from multiple public databases and indexes related to Chinese global finance and recipient countries' electoral democracy, freedom, and data protection and privacy status. In this report, we analyze this quantitative dataset—adding qualitative country case studies based on interviews and social media analysis—to examine the distribution, technology, financing, and data safety aspects of China's AI exports. Our specific research questions are as follows:

- How have AI exports financed by the Chinese government changed between 2000 and 2017 (the latest year for which data were available)?
- Which countries, industry sectors, and social domains are the most affected by China's AI exports?
- What factors make China's AI exports competitive in the developing world?
- How does the public in recipient countries perceive China's AI exports?

When trying to identify China's AI export projects, we differentiated between two AI project categories. One category contains *AI application projects* that directly use AI technologies, such as facial recognition, speech recognition, and algorithms that facilitate medical diagnosis. The other contains *AI infrastructure projects*, such as building data centers, connecting 5G network technology, laying fiber optical cables, training in AI technology, and installing AI hardware (such as closed-circuit television cameras) that provide the necessary platform for AI deployment.

---

[1] Jun Mai, "Technology Key to China's Vision for the Future as a World Leading Power," *South China Morning Post*, March 6, 2021; David Barboza and John Markoff, "Power in Numbers: China Aims for High-Tech Primacy," *New York Times*, December 5, 2011.

Key Findings

Trends in AI Exports Financed by the Chinese Government Between 2000 and 2017

We identified 155 AI projects committed by China's official-sector institutions over the period between 2000 and 2017. These projects consisted of 94 AI application projects and 61 AI infrastructure projects across 51 countries in Asia, Africa, Eastern Europe, the Caribbean, and Latin America. These publicly funded AI exports from China escalated after 2005, increasing fivefold from 2005 to 2011, and doubling again between 2012 and 2017. The initial rapid growth can be attributed to China's publicly financed AI infrastructure projects that dominated the market. In contrast, the later years saw an increasing reliance on AI applications, and China's publicly funded projects experienced relatively slower growth.

Three Factors Associated with China's Progression in AI Exports to the Developing World

We identified the following three factors that characterize China's AI exports to the developing world:

- *An integrated approach to technology exports.* China provides AI application projects and AI infrastructure projects, such as integrated data centers, fiber optic networks, installation of surveillance cameras, and related hardware.
- *Affordability.* Chinese products aim for low- and mid-price tiers. This approach applies to the projects implemented for the host country, such as fiber optic networks, and to downstream devices and software that use AI-generated information, such as handsets and operating systems. The result is a systemwide Chinese presence that runs the gamut from large projects that use and generate AI-enabling datasets to smaller interventions that involve the provision of devices.
- *Flexibility in operations.* China's AI projects are often tailored to the recipient countries' requirements, come with financing packages, and offer timeline modifications as needed. Such flexibility is rooted in China's strategic focus, which includes a willingness to engage with fragile political environments, regardless of regime type. However, this practice can also give rise to concerns and criticism.

Countries, Industry Sectors, and Social Domains Affected by China's AI Exports

China's AI exports are concentrated in low- and middle-income countries (LMIC) that are China's Belt and Road Initiative partner countries across Asia, Africa, and Latin America.

Most of these countries fall under non-liberal democratic categories: electoral democracy,[2] electoral autocracy, or closed autocracy.

The sectoral allocation shows that AI technologies relate to Safe City or Smart City, e-government, communication, and medical imaging projects. In comparing the allocation of Chinese AI projects with non-AI development projects, we found no clear preferences toward specific political regimes except that electoral democracies import more AI infrastructure projects and closed autocracies were more likely to import AI for health and communications than for e-government use. Free countries (as defined by Freedom House) import a bigger share of AI infrastructure projects (30 percent) than they do with AI application projects (23 percent) or non-AI projects (18 percent).

Most of the countries receiving China's financed AI projects were still formulating their data protection policies as of the end of 2017. We found that only 15 percent of the projects in the communications sector and 24 percent of the projects in the government sector landed in countries that have robust data protection laws. However, compared with non-AI projects funded by China's development funding, a much bigger share of China's AI exports landed in countries that have robust data protection laws. This could mean that countries that have more experience with using AI are more likely to adopt data protection laws and are more likely to import AI technology from China and other countries.

Perspectives on China's AI Exports in Recipient Countries

Perception of China's AI exports is multifaceted, differing considerably among the administration, medical professionals, and the public in recipient countries. Administrators and medical professionals favor China's AI exports to their countries, viewing them as helping meet national needs. The public's sentiment toward AI exports generally tends to be more negative, largely driven by concerns over their governments' lack of capability for effectively using AI technologies while ensuring data safety. A particular cause for dissatisfaction lies in the perceived inefficiency of the Safe City initiative in crime reduction.

Recommendations

Our findings will be useful for stakeholders interested in understanding the emerging global risks and opportunities of China's AI exports to LMIC. The stakeholders include policymakers and civil society in host countries, donor country policymakers, international foundations, and multilateral organizations for development. Our key findings showed that (1) China's development-financed AI exports were concentrated in developing countries that were interested in AI technology in Safe City or Smart City projects, e-government, and medical

---

[2] *Electoral democracy* is a non-liberal category because liberal democracy countries have individual and minority rights, equality before the law, and executive restraint by the legislature and the courts.

use across different regime types; (2) Chinese AI infrastructure projects preceded AI application projects; and (3) many recipient countries had not set robust AI data safety laws, or the laws lack enforcement mechanisms. For these concerns, highlighted by our in-depth public interviews in two of the recipient countries, we offer the following recommendations:

- **Policymakers and civil society in recipient countries should ensure transparency with AI imports, particularly for those imports used in governance and communication projects.** Such policies should meet the best procurement standards and should ensure the adequate availability to civil society of information on the outcomes and impacts of these projects. Countries can also promote accountability by setting and following a national AI-technology-adoption strategy with a realistic expectation of AI's ability to fight crime. Donor countries and agencies (including the United States) can support recipient countries' governments and civil society to achieve the desired transparency.
- **Host governments' regulatory branches should aim to continue building data safety policies and implementation processes. To support such policies, civil society's capacity to support data safety measures needs to be strengthened.** Donors should conduct thorough assessments of existing data and AI policies within recipient countries and collaborate with recipient countries to establish robust monitoring and evaluation systems. Failing in good AI governance will lead to public distrust of AI imports.
- **Donor countries should help build local AI literacy and prepare to provide ancillary support for the AI application ecosystem.** Building AI literacy involves educating the younger generation on AI, fostering local AI talent through education and training, supporting local tech entrepreneurship, and creating a conducive regulatory environment for innovation. Donors or other investors should help by providing ancillary services, such as AI literacy programs, mentorship, market linkages, and infrastructure development, in addition to technology transfers.

Contents

APPENDIXES

Figures and Tables

Figures

Tables

CHAPTER 1

Introduction

The first two decades of the 21st century have witnessed a significant transformation in the global landscape, with China emerging as the second-largest economy. This economic ascent has been followed by a surge in scientific research and development as China works to close the technology gap with the West. In doing so, Chinese leaders hope to achieve a long-nurtured grand vision in which China assumes the mantle of global technology leadership. This ambition has ignited a strong political will in China to invest in artificial intelligence (AI) applications for national security, economic development, and societal welfare. The blueprint for AI development, such as the State Council's New Generation Artificial Intelligence Development Plan,[1] sets out to advance China's domestic AI development and position China as a critical player in the global technological arena.

China has made it clear that it perceives AI as a critical component of its rise as a world power, but it is by no means the only country that holds this view. Many nations understand that the first country to harness AI technology fully will have the advantage of dictating the standards and rules in the digital world, thereby gaining considerable geopolitical influence. In the past two decades, AI development has advanced significantly and now spans from complex algorithms and machine learning models to highly sophisticated systems capable of natural language processing, image recognition, and autonomous decisionmaking. Furthermore, AI's rapid evolution has reshaped industries from health care to finance to transportation and raised fundamental questions about ethics, privacy, and the future of work in an increasingly automated world. We are witnessing a global race: Many nations are investing heavily in AI development and talents and are encouraging AI integration across industry sectors to gain benefits and strategic edges.

In the context of the economic and technological boom of the past decade, China's Belt and Road Initiative (BRI) emerged as a whole-of-government endeavor to enhance the nation's geoeconomic and geopolitical footprint on the global map. Envisioned as a modern-day Silk Road, the BRI opens avenues for Chinese factories to connect to Eurasia's markets more efficiently. The BRI also helps bridge the gaping infrastructure chasm prevalent in emerging markets in Southeast Asia, Latin America, and Africa, thus claiming to offer mutually beneficial prospects for both China and its partner nations—hence, a successful South-South col-

---

[1] Graham Webster, Rogier Creemers, Elsa Kania, and Paul Triolo, "Full Translation: China's 'New Generation Artificial Intelligence Development Plan' (2017)," webpage, DigiChina, August 1, 2017.

laboration. With annual commitments of over $85 billion from 2013 to 2021, China has been the world's largest provider of development financing and has outspent the United States on a two-to-one basis.[2] China's official-sector financing mechanism placed the Chinese government at the helm, masterminding this ambitious global investment blueprint.

The BRI and its newer Digital Silk Road spinoff are convenient platforms to allow China to scout opportunities to expand its technology's uptake in new overseas markets. Nations—including several U.S. allies—increasingly rely on China's technology infrastructure.[3] AI technology, as a tool to enhance governance and service delivery, is often integrated into the Digital Silk Road initiatives of the Smart City and Safe City. China's AI exports will likely continue to grow and influence the global AI technology–related supply chain, trade, technology standards, and regulatory systems.

Although there is an increasing amount of research and analysis on China's domestic AI development ecosystems, regulations, and drivers,[4] China's strategy of using overseas development finance to support AI exports remains an elusive aspect of its global outreach efforts. These projects can be particularly hard to trace because Beijing does not participate in any development finance transparency initiatives, such as the Organisation for Economic Co-operation and Development's (OECD's) Common Reporting Standard or the International Aid Transparency Initiative.[5] The details of what Chinese official-sector financiers have achieved globally and where and how they have achieved it are largely unknown outside official Chinese circles. This has raised concerns about these exports. For example, a recent study showed that facial recognition technology dominates the high-technology goods and services that China exports to autocracies and weak democracies.[6] This could have implications for how China's AI exports might affect global democracy and human rights protections.

---

[2] Ammar A. Malik, Bradley Parks, Brooke Russell, Joyce Jiahui Lin, Katherine Walsh, Kyra Solomon, Sheng Zhang, Thai-Binh Elston, and Seth Goodman, *Banking on the Belt and Road: Insights from a New Global Dataset of 13,427 Chinese Development Projects*, AidData at William & Mary, September 29, 2021.

[3] Mark Montgomery and Eric Sayers, "Don't Let China Take over the Cloud—US National Security Depends on It," *The Hill*, November 13, 2023.

[4] Matt Sheehan, *China's AI Regulations and How They Get Made*, Carnegie Endowment for International Peace, July 10, 2023; Ngor Luong and Zachary Arnold, *China's Artificial Intelligence Industry Alliance*, Center for Security and Emerging Technology, May 2021; Jeffery Ding, "China's Current Capabilities, Policies, and Industrial Ecosystem in AI," testimony before the U.S.-China Economic and Security Review Commission Hearing on Technology, Trade, and Military-Civil Fusion: China's Pursuit of Artificial Intelligence, New Materials, and New Energy, June 7, 2019.

[5] Pierre Mandon and Martha Tesfaye Woldemichael, "Has Chinese Aid Benefitted Recipient Countries?" Brookings Institution, April 6, 2023.

[6] Martin Beraja, Andrew Kao, David Y. Yang, and Noam Yuchtman, *Exporting the Surveillance State via Trade in AI*, Brookings Institution, January 2023.

Focus of This Report

Our report is part of a larger project to better understand China's AI exports. We first produced an innovative dataset—China's AI Exports Database (CAIED)[7]—and interactive maps by combining selected portions of AidData's Global Chinese Development Finance (GCDF) Dataset version 2.0.[8] Details on CAIED can be found in a companion report and are summarized in Appendix A.[9] In this report, we focus on analyzing these new data to examine the characteristics of the distribution, technology, sector, public finance, and data safety aspects of China's AI exports. We also conducted qualitative analyses to assess how recipient nations' public and policymakers view China's AI exports. Specifically, we asked the following questions:

- How have AI exports financed by the Chinese government changed between 2000 and 2017?[10]
- What factors make China's AI exports competitive in the developing world?
- Which countries, industry sectors, and social domains are the most affected by China's AI exports?
- How does the public in recipient countries perceive China's AI exports?

The answers to these questions will allow us to offer informed policy recommendations that are valuable to policymakers from countries and international organizations that support the transfer of AI technology and to AI regulatory agencies and civil society in the countries that are receiving AI technology transfers.

---

[7] Jennifer Bouey, Lynn Hu, Keller Scholl, William Marcellino, Stacey Yi, Rafiq Dossani, James Gazis, Ammar A. Malik, Kyra Solomon, Sheng Zhang, and Andy Shufer, *China's AI Exports Database (CAIED)*, RAND Corporation, TL-A2696-1, 2023a.

[8] AidData, AidData's Global Chinese Development Finance Dataset, version 2.0, database, September 29, 2021; Samantha Custer, Axel Dreher, Thai-Binh Elston, Andreas Fuchs, Siddharta Ghose, Joyce Jiahul Lin, Ammar A. Malik, Bradley C. Parks, Brooke Russell, Kyra Solomon, Austin Strange, Michael J. Tierney, Katherine Walsh, Lincoln Zaleski, and Sheng Zhang, *Tracking Chinese Development Finance: An Application of AidData's TUFF 2.0 Methodology*, AidData at William & Mary, September 29, 2021; Axel Dreher, Andreas Fuchs, Bradley Parks, Austin Strange, and Michael J. Tierney, *Banking on Beijing: The Aims and Impacts of China's Overseas Development Program*, Cambridge University Press, 2022.

[9] Jennifer Bouey, Lynn Hu, Keller Scholl, William Marcellino, James Gazis, Ammar A. Malik, Kyra Solomon, Sheng Zhang, and Andy Shufer, *China's AI Exports: Developing a Tool to Track Chinese Development Finance in the Global South—Technical Documentation*, RAND Corporation, RR-A2696-1, 2023b.

[10] RAND researchers collaborated with AidData to create a first-of-its-kind interactive tool, showing China's AI influence in the developing world. The publications in this series are the first published studies to use quantitative and qualitative metrics to examine China's AI technology exports. The analysis summarized in this series reflects data available to the research team from AidData's GCDF 2.0, which covers the years 2000–2017. An updated GCDF 3.0 was made available in November 2023, and the research team is working on analyzing the new dataset, which extends the time horizon covered through 2021.

Approach

We first created CAIED, keeping the projects identified as China's AI application projects or AI infrastructure projects (details can be found in the companion report and Appendix A[11]). In short, *AI application projects* are defined as projects that use AI technologies, such as speech recognition, facial recognition, natural language processing, deep learning, intelligent robotics, and automatic decisionmaking. *AI infrastructure projects* are defined as projects that enable the development of AI, such as building AI infrastructure (e.g., data centers, fiber optics, code-division multiple access [CDMA]/radio stations implemented after 2012), and human capacity-building. We also included projects that might facilitate AI implementation, such as container scanners, seismic monitoring, closed-circuit television (CCTV) cameras, and medical imaging that gather data for processing machine learning models. *AI projects* are defined as AI application projects or AI infrastructure projects. *Non-AI projects* are defined as all AidData's GCDF 2.0 projects from countries contained in CAIED that are neither AI application nor AI infrastructure projects. These projects can belong to various sectors, such as transport and storage, energy, and water supply and sanitation.

We applied a combination of quantitative and qualitative analyses in this report. The quantitative analysis is based on CAIED. This database combines data from several data sources: AidData's GCDF dataset,[12] the Electoral Democracy Index from Our World in Data,[13] the Countries and Territories data file from Freedom House,[14] the Data Protection and Privacy Legislation Worldwide database from the United Nations Conference on Trade and Development,[15] and the Data Protection Laws of the World database from DLA Piper.[16] Descriptions of these indexes can be found in Appendix A.

For the qualitative research component, we built two country case studies by documenting public sentiment on China's AI exports and conducting social media analysis. Details of the methodology can be found in Appendix B.

Report Organization

The remainder of this report consists of four chapters. In Chapter 2, we present our analysis of the distribution of China's AI application and AI infrastructure export projects over time across global geographic areas, by industry sectors and technologies, and by recipient coun-

---

[11] Bouey et al., 2023b.

[12] Custer et al., 2021; Dreher et al., 2022.

[13] Bastian Herre, Esteban Ortiz-Ospina, and Max Roser, "Democracy," webpage, Our World in Data, 2013.

[14] Freedom House, "Country and Territory Ratings and Statuses, 1973–2023," spreadsheet, undated-a.

[15] United Nations Conference on Trade and Development, Data Protection and Privacy Legislation Worldwide, database, December 14, 2021.

[16] DLA Piper, Data Protection Laws of the World, database, undated.

tries' governance regimes and data policy status. In Chapter 3, we present our findings on China's AI that we gained from in-depth public interviews in two countries—Kenya and Pakistan—and from Brandwatch sentiment analysis of local Twitter data.[17] In Chapter 4, we synthesize findings from the quantitative and qualitative approaches to answer the four research questions we listed above and highlight the limitations of the current methodology. In Chapter 5, we provide policy recommendations for both AI recipient and AI donor countries and organizations. In Appendix A, we describe the key constructs that we used in the quantitative analysis; in Appendix B, we provide additional information on the methodologies that we used in this study.

---

[17] We collected this data prior to Twitter being renamed X.

CHAPTER 2

China's AI Exports: Global Distributions over Time

In this chapter, we present the results of our analyses using CAIED. The analysis considers the distribution of AI applications and AI infrastructure projects across different geographic areas over time, by industry sectors and technologies, and by recipient countries' governance regimes and data policy status. By coupling China's overseas development financing information with data on countries' governance styles and data policy indexes, we can evaluate the association, if any, between the proliferation of Chinese AI technology and shifts in democracy and data safety metrics.

Specifically, the analysis in this chapter sheds light on

- the proportion of China's development financing that focuses on AI versus other development priorities
- whether countries' adoption of China's AI technologies globally boosts China's dominance in the markets of certain technology sectors
- whether China's AI exports are more likely to be adopted by authoritarian regimes to strengthen surveillance or control.

China's AI Exports Increased over Time

At the time of this writing in 2023, there were 155 projects in CAIED, consisting of 94 AI application projects and 61 AI infrastructure projects during the period from 2000 to 2017. These projects represent a small fraction of China's overseas portfolio of aid- and credit-financed projects that were recorded in the source data. Altogether, AidData's GCDF 2.0 dataset, Global Chinese Military Finance dataset, and Global Huawei Finance dataset capture 11,394 projects supported by grants and loans from China worth a total of $853.7 billion.[1] The 155 AI projects in CAIED thus accounted for only 1.4 percent of the total number

---

[1] Custer et al., 2021; Dreher et al., 2022. Of the 11,394 projects, 10,849 are from the GCDF 2.0 dataset, 153 are from the Huawei dataset, and 392 are from the military dataset. We filtered the 11,394 projects from the overall 13,427 development projects in AidData's GCDF 2.0 dataset by using the Recommended_for_ Aggregates variable to exclude pledges that were never formally committed, canceled projects, suspended

and 0.5 percent (or $4.5 billion in constant 2017 U.S. dollars) of the total commitment value of China's official-sector development finance exports between 2000 and 2017.

All 155 projects in the dataset were primarily funded by loans and grants from the Chinese government. One hundred projects (65 percent) were Chinese official aid projects, and 52 were funded by loans, such as export buyer credits, interest-free loans, concessional loans, or export supplier credits from China. The remaining three projects did not have sufficient information to classify a flow type and were coded as "unclear." No statistically significant association was found between AI application versus AI infrastructure projects and the different types of funding (grants versus loans).

Figure 2.1 shows that the number of AI application projects exceeded that of AI infrastructure projects and that both steadily increased during this period. There were few AI projects (i.e., AI applications and AI infrastructure) before 2005, but these projects increased between 2006 and 2012 and reached higher volume after 2012. Figure 2.1 illustrates a robust linear relationship between project numbers and year, and the model explains more than 90 percent of the changes in annual project numbers. The noticeable increase in AI projects (slope = 1.1, where slope represents the average increased number of projects over a year) can be broken down to the faster growth in AI applications (slope = 0.7) and a slower growth rate

FIGURE 2.1

China's Development-Funded AI Projects Counts, 2000–2017

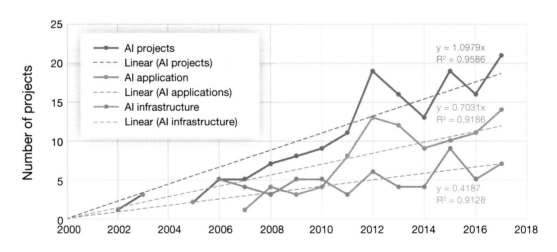

NOTE: AI projects consist of both AI application and AI infrastructure projects.
SOURCES: Features information from CAIED and AidData's GCDF 2.0 dataset and constituent Huawei and military datasets.

projects, or projects that would double-count our financial totals or project counts (or both). Nineteen percent of projects are missing the commitment value; therefore, we did not use the amount in U.S. dollars as an indicator in our analysis. Using project counts as an indicator of AI applications in the country is preferred; however, we cannot differentiate whether a supplement project is an independent one or part of the previous project. This can result in the overcounting of some projects.

in AI infrastructure (slope = 0.4). This observation aligns with the logical dependence of AI applications on a robust infrastructure.

Furthermore, the slower growth observed after 2012 (slope = 0.45 for all AI projects after 2012 compared with 1.1 before 2012) can be attributed to the fact that the growth was increasingly driven by AI applications rather than infrastructure, and the Chinese *public* development-funded AI application projects were less competitive against other competitors compared with the advantages enjoyed by the public-funded AI infrastructure projects.

China's AI Export Projects Were Concentrated in Three Sectors and Four Technologies

Figures 2.2 and 2.3 illustrate the trend of AI project counts by sector and technology category. Among the 155 AI projects, 54 (35 percent) went to the health sector, 39 (25 percent) were government and civil society projects,[2] and another 38 (25 percent) were allocated to communication technologies. On average, the 30 health-sector projects cost $11 million per project. The remaining 24 projects were allocated to the following sectors: trade, education, disaster prevention, emergency response, other social infrastructure, transport, industry and mining, agriculture, and other multisector projects. We included health-sector AI projects in the study because most medical imaging technologies after the mid-2000s use AI apps to enhance diagnosis accuracy and reduce radiation exposure to patients. The advanced biometric capture and image processing used in medical imaging technology is a critical component of AI development.

On technology domains, the majority of AI exported by China was medical imaging technology used in both the health and crisis management sectors, which consisted of 60 (39 percent) of the 155 exports. Thirty projects (19 percent) were for Safe City or Smart City projects, and 24 (15 percent) were for e-government projects. Safe City or Smart City projects cost an average of $61 million, and e-government projects cost $53 million. The remaining 41 projects (26 percent) fall into the technology categories of advanced computing and data storage (13 projects), remote sensing and seismic monitoring (12 projects), security scanners (nine projects), unmanned vehicles (four projects), and other (three projects).

---

[2] The sector names are based on the OECD's sector categorization scheme (OECD, "DAC and CRS Code Lists," webpage, undated). The government and civil society sector includes the following OECD Development Assistance Committee (DAC) 5 codes: government and civil society—general (150) and conflict, peace and security (152). The Creditor Reporting System (CRS) codes included in government and civil society—general (150) are public sector policy and administrative management (15110), public finance management (15111), decentralisation and support to subnational government (15112), anti-corruption organisations and institutions (15113), domestic revenue mobilization (15114), public procurement (15125), legal and judicial development (15130), macroeconomic policy (15142), democratic participation and civil society (15150), elections (15151), legislatures and political parties (15152), media and free flow of information (15153), human rights (15160), women's equality organisations and institutions (15170), ending violence against women and girls (15180), and facilitation of orderly, safe, regular and responsible migration and mobility (15190).

FIGURE 2.2

AI Project Counts by Sector, 2000–2017

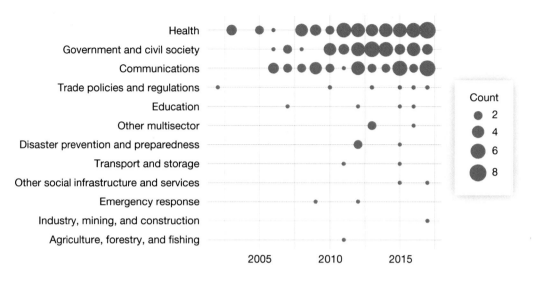

NOTE: AI projects consist of both AI application and AI infrastructure projects.
SOURCE: Features information from CAIED.

FIGURE 2.3

AI Project Counts by Technology Category, 2000–2017

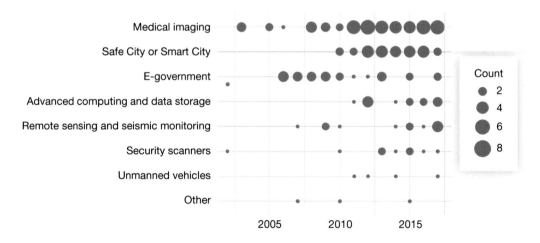

NOTE: AI projects consist of both AI application and AI infrastructure projects.
SOURCE: Features information from CAIED.

China's AI Exports Span the Globe Without Regime-Bias

Global Distribution of China's AI Exports

In the interactive world map, users can view all 155 AI application and AI infrastructure projects exported from China between 2000 and 2017. Figure 2.4 provides a screenshot of the interactive map that shows the geographic distribution of China's AI projects in terms of counts and commitment values. The height of each spike reflects the count of identified projects per country, and the intensity of color for each spike shows the total transaction amount for all projects in the selected country. Using the interactive map, users can choose to view both AI application and AI infrastructure projects, just AI application projects, or just AI infrastructure projects by applying the filter on the top left of the world map. Table 2.1. shows the top recipient countries by project counts and commitment value as reflected on the world map.

TABLE 2.1

Top Ten Recipient Countries by Project Counts and Commitment Value

Rank	Rank by Project Counts	Rank by Commitment Value
1	Pakistan (five AI application and four AI infrastructure projects)	Zambia ($534 million)
2	Uganda (three AI application and four AI infrastructure projects)	Pakistan ($533 million)
3	Guyana (four AI application and two AI infrastructure projects)	Nigeria ($483 million)
4	Cabo Verde (one AI application and four AI infrastructure projects)	Ghana ($309 million)
5	Kenya (four AI application and one AI infrastructure project)	Kenya ($283 million)
6	Egypt (four AI application and one AI infrastructure project)	Bangladesh ($282 million)
7	Samoa (two AI application and three AI infrastructure projects)	Senegal ($250 million)
8	Ecuador (two AI application and three AI infrastructure projects)	Cameroon ($243 million)
9	Cameroon (two AI application and two AI infrastructure projects)	Uganda ($147 million)
10	Senegal (zero AI application and four AI infrastructure projects)	Mozambique ($147 million)

SOURCE: Features information from CAIED.

11

FIGURE 2.4

Screenshot of Interactive World Map from CAIED

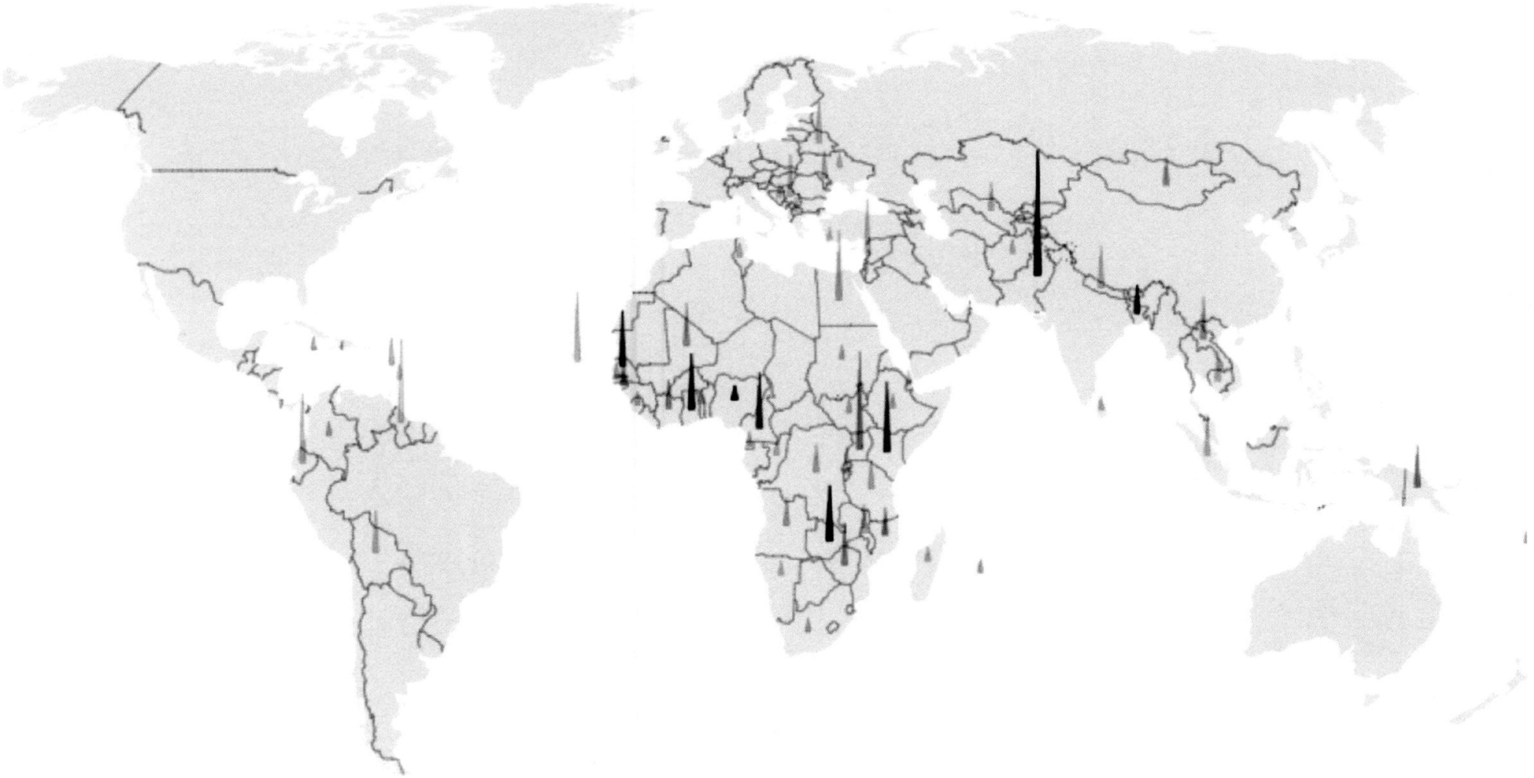

NOTE: The interactive map can be accessed at www.rand.org/t/TLA2696-1

No Apparent Bias in the Distribution of AI and Non-AI Projects by Country Regime

Our World in Data's Regimes of the World database distinguishes four types of political systems: closed autocracies, electoral autocracies, electoral democracies, and liberal democracies.[3] Closed autocracies do not allow citizens to choose the chief executive or legislature through multiparty elections. Electoral autocracies allow citizens to choose the chief executive and legislature in multiparty elections, but citizens lack certain freedoms, such as the freedoms of association and expression, that make elections meaningful. Electoral democracies give citizens the right to elect the chief executive and legislature through free, fair, and meaningful multiparty elections. Liberal democracies have electoral democracy with individual and minority rights, equality before the law, and executive restraint by the legislature and courts.[4]

To understand how these regimes are distributed in the world where China AI exports landed, we looked into the regime distribution among African countries in 2017. We found that 10.7 percent of African countries (six countries) were closed autocracies, 50.0 percent (28 countries) had an electoral autocracy system, 33.9 percent (19 countries) had electoral democracy, and 5.3 percent (three countries) were liberal democracies.[5] China's overseas project non-AI distribution follows this proportion distribution (Figure 2.5). The global distribution of regimes shows a higher percentage of liberal democracies in comparison, which suggests that a significant portion of China's overseas finance is directed toward developing countries.

When we compare the distribution of AI projects (project counts) going to different regimes with the distribution of non-AI projects going to different regimes (indexed in 2022), we do not see much difference, especially between the distribution of AI projects and non-AI projects. After separating AI infrastructure and AI applications, we found that AI infrastructure projects were slightly more likely to land in electoral democracy nations (Figure 2.5).

Also, if we look at the distribution of projects exported to countries with different regime types in the top three sectors for AI exports, we do not see much difference between the AI and non-AI projects (see Figure 2.6).

---

[3] Herre, Ortiz-Ospina, and Roser, 2013.

[4] Bastian Herre, "The 'Regimes of the World' Data: How Do Researchers Measure Democracy?" webpage, Our World in Data, December 2, 2021.

[5] The statistics for the political regime types of African countries in 2017 were abstracted from the Democracy Data Explorer (Regimes of the World dataset) at the Our World in Data website (Herre, Ortiz-Ospina, and Roser, 2013).

FIGURE 2.5

Percentages of AI Applications, AI Infrastructure, and Non-AI Projects Exported to Countries with Different Regime Types

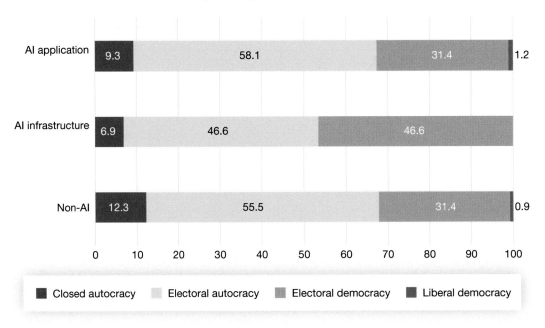

SOURCES: Features information from CAIED and AidData's GCDF 2.0 dataset and constituent Huawei and military datasets.

NOTE: A chi-square test was performed between the AI projects and non-AI projects, and no statistically significant difference was found between the two samples. When we exclude AidData's Huawei and military datasets from the analysis, the difference is still insignificant. AI projects consist of both AI application and AI infrastructure projects but do not include the 11 countries that have no data (N = 144). Non-AI projects only consist of projects from countries that are in CAIED (N = 6,884).

FIGURE 2.6

Percentages of AI and Non-AI Projects Exported to Countries with Different Regime Types in the Top Three Sectors

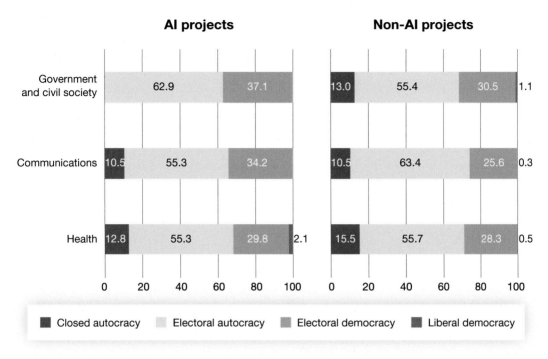

SOURCES: Features information from CAIED and AidData's GCDF 2.0 dataset and constituent Huawei and military datasets.

NOTE: A chi-square test was performed between the AI and non-AI projects, and no statistically significant difference was found between the two samples in all three sectors. AI projects consist of AI application and AI infrastructure projects that have available political regime data: health ($n = 47$), communications ($n = 38$), government and civil society ($n = 35$).

China's AI Projects Are More Likely to Be Implemented in Free Countries

State or nonstate actors can have an impact on individual liberties, such as the ability to vote, freedom of expression, and equality before the law. Through its yearly *Freedom in the World* report, Freedom House rates the availability of political rights and civil liberties in 210 nations and territories.[6] Using the Freedom House ratings, if we compare the distribution of AI projects (project counts) going to countries with different freedom levels and the distribution of non-AI projects going to countries with different freedom levels, we find that China's AI projects were more likely to be exported to free countries (see Figure 2.7).

---

[6] Freedom House, "Freedom in the World," webpage, undated-b.

FIGURE 2.7

Percentages of AI Application, AI Infrastructure, and Non-AI Projects Exported to Countries with Different Human Rights Ratings

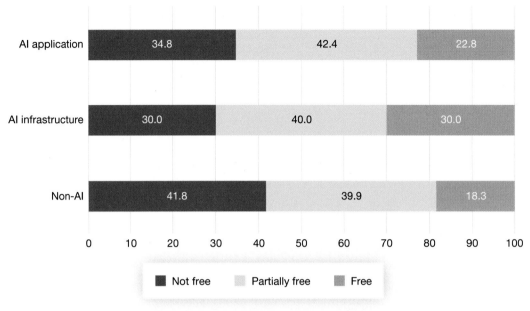

SOURCES: Features information from CAIED and AidData's GCDF 2.0 dataset and constituent Huawei and military datasets.

NOTE: A chi-square test was performed between the AI projects and non-AI projects, and the difference between the two samples was statistically significantly different (p-value = 0.027). When we exclude AidData's Huawei and military datasets from the analysis, the difference is still significant (p-value = 0.009). AI projects consist of both AI application and AI infrastructure projects but do not include the three countries that have no data (N = 152). Non-AI projects only consist of projects from countries that are in CAIED (N = 6,978).

When we look at the distribution of projects into different regime types by sector (Figure 2.8), we see different patterns of distribution between AI and non-AI projects, especially in the government and civil society sector, in which 60 percent of the Chinese AI projects landed in countries that are partly free, while more than 40 percent of the non-AI projects landed in countries that are not free. For projects in the health sector, the share of AI health projects that exported to free countries (29 percent) is two times bigger than the share of non-AI health projects that exported to free countries (15 percent).

The Association of China's AI Exports with Some Forms of Data Policies in Recipient Countries

Data protection laws refer to the legal framework governing the collection, storage, use, and transfer of personal data. These laws aim to protect the privacy rights of a country's citizens by regulating how organizations handle personal data while also giving individuals rights over their own data. When looking at countries' data protection law status and level, we can

FIGURE 2.8

Percentages of AI and Non-AI Projects Exported to Countries with Different Human Rights Ratings in the Top Three Sectors

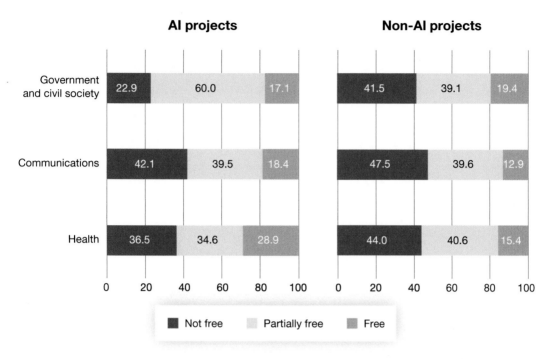

SOURCES: Features information from CAIED and AidData's GCDF 2.0 dataset and constituent Huawei and military datasets.

NOTE: A chi-square test was performed between the AI projects and non-AI projects, and a statistically significant difference was found between the two samples in the government and civil society and health sectors (*p*-values = 0.037 and 0.036, respectively). AI projects contain both AI application and AI infrastructure projects that have available human rights ratings data: *n* = 52 for health, *n* = 38 for communications, and *n* = 35 for government and civil society.

see that many countries already have data protection legislation in place,[7] although AI projects are found to be more likely to be exported to countries with existing data protection legislation than non-AI projects (see Figure 2.9). Within each of the top three sectors, a higher percentage of AI projects than non-AI projects were exported to countries that have existing data protection legislation (see Figure 2.10).

---

[7] United Nations Conference on Trade and Development, 2021.

FIGURE 2.9

Percentages of AI Application, AI Infrastructure, and Non-AI Projects Exported to Countries with Different Data Protection Law Status

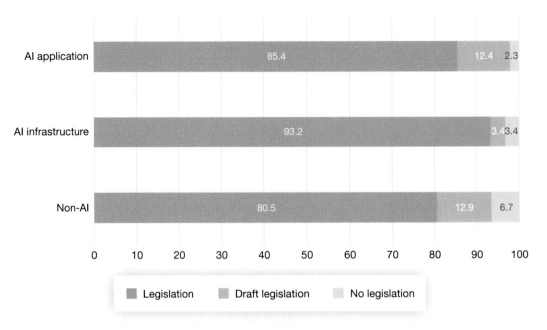

SOURCES: Features information from CAIED and AidData's GCDF 2.0 dataset and constituent Huawei and military datasets.

NOTE: A chi-square test was performed between the AI projects and non-AI projects, and the difference between the two samples was statistically significantly different (p-value = 0.039). When we exclude Huawei and military datasets from the analysis, the difference is no longer significant (p-value = 0.074). AI projects consist of both AI application and AI infrastructure projects but do not include the seven countries that have no data (N = 148). Non-AI projects only consist of projects from countries that are in CAIED (N = 6,724).

FIGURE 2.10

Percentages of AI and Non-AI Projects Exported to Countries with Different Data Protection Law Status in the Top Three Sectors

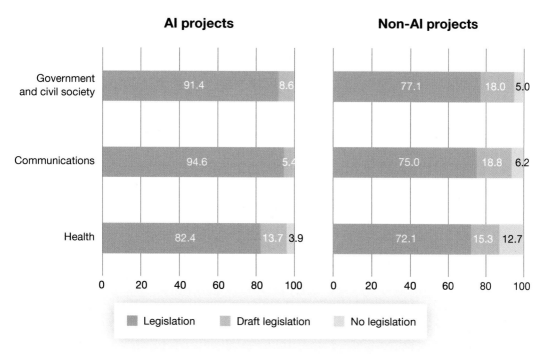

SOURCES: Features information from CAIED and AidData's GCDF 2.0 dataset and constituent Huawei and military datasets.

NOTE: A chi-square test was performed between the AI projects and non-AI projects, and a statistically significant difference was found between the two samples in the communications sector (*p*-value = 0.025). AI projects consist of both AI application and AI infrastructure projects with data on data protection law status: *n* = 51 for health, *n* = 37 for communications, *n* = 35 for government and civil society.

If we look at the data protection stringency level,[8] 20 percent of AI infrastructure projects went into countries with robust data security laws, which is more than twice as big as the percentage of non-AI projects that went into countries with robust data security laws (see Figure 2.11). Although there was no large difference between the overall distribution patterns of AI and non-AI projects within the top three sectors, a much bigger share of AI projects from the government and civil society and communications sectors were exported to countries with robust data protection laws (see Figure 2.12).

---

8   DLA Piper, undated.

FIGURE 2.11

Percentages of AI Application, AI Infrastructure, and Non-AI Projects Exported to Countries with Different Data Protection Law Levels

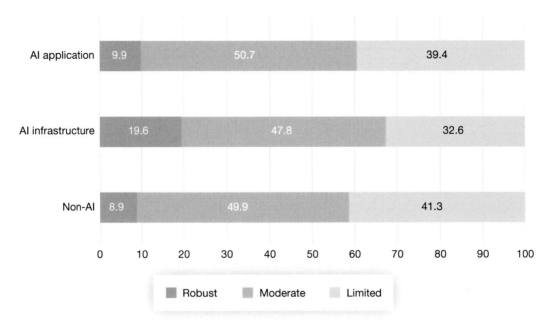

SOURCES: Features information from CAIED and AidData's GCDF 2.0 dataset and constituent Huawei and military datasets.

NOTE: A chi-square test was performed between the AI and non-AI projects, and no statistically significant difference was found between the two samples. The difference is still insignificant when we exclude Huawei and military datasets from the analysis. AI projects consist of both AI application and AI infrastructure projects but do not include the 38 countries that have no data ($N = 117$). Non-AI projects consist of projects from countries that are in CAIED ($N = 5,317$).

FIGURE 2.12

Percentages of AI and Non-AI Projects Exported to Countries with Different Data Protection Law Levels in the Top Three Sectors

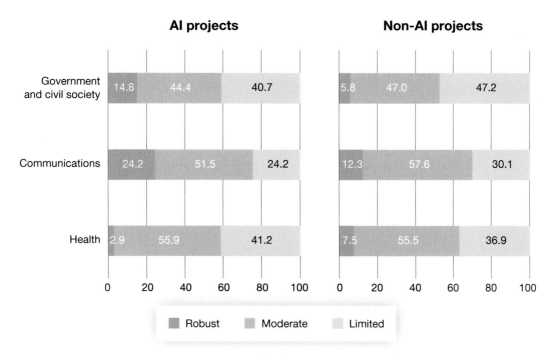

SOURCES: Features information from CAIED and AidData's GCDF 2.0 dataset and constituent Huawei and military datasets.
NOTE: A chi-square test was performed between the AI projects and non-AI projects, and no statistically significant difference was found between the two samples in all three sectors. AI projects consist of both AI application and AI infrastructure projects with data on data protection law level: $n = 34$ for health, $n = 33$ for communications, and $n = 27$ for government and civil society.

In summary, between the years 2000 and 2017, China AI exports represented only a small fraction of the country's wide-ranging overseas initiatives. However, an emergence and growth of AI projects were noticeable after 2005, accelerating rapidly from 2006 to 2012, before eventually reaching a plateau. These 155 projects were predominantly centered in the health, government and civil society, and communications sectors that most eagerly absorbed these AI advancements. In terms of geographical distribution, the impact of China's AI export projects was mainly felt in Africa, Asia, and Latin America. We compared AI projects and non-AI projects by countries' regime type, freedom status, and data protection law status. We found that more AI projects were exported to free countries and countries with data protection legislation and robust data protection laws.

CHAPTER 3

Country Case Studies: Kenya and Pakistan

Complementary to the analysis on the distribution of China's AI projects, we assessed public opinions toward China's AI exports through subject-matter expert in-depth interviews and Brandwatch Twitter sentiment analysis. Details of the methodology can be found in Appendix B.

Public Attitudes Toward China's AI Technologies in Recipient Countries

According to our analysis, most English-language Twitter users from top recipient countries were neutral when discussing China's AI technologies from 2021 to 2022 (see Figure 3.1).[1] Ugandan and Zambian users were most likely to express negative feelings about Chinese AI (43 percent and 32 percent negative sentiments, respectively). A closer look into the emotions associated with Chinese AI shows that Ugandan social media users were almost equally distributed in expressing joy (22 percent) and disgust (26 percent), while nearly one-third (31 percent) expressed fear (see Figure 3.2). The emotions that dominated in Zambia were anger (26 percent), fear (27 percent), and sadness (27 percent). The data for the two nations that we chose for an in-depth case study—Kenya and Pakistan—show that social media users in those two nations expressed sentiments that were, on average, similar to those in other nations and were predominately *fear* and *sadness*.

Naturally, these general sentiments can be hard to interpret without understanding their context. Therefore, we conducted in-depth key informant interviews in Kenya and Pakistan to gain a better understanding of how the public in those countries thinks about AI, China's AI exports, and the impact of AI on different sectors of their societies. These countries were selected because they received the most Chinese AI exports by project counts and financial

---

[1] We conducted our analysis using the Brandwatch Consumer Research platform social media tool and used English Twitter data from January 1, 2021, through December 31, 2022. The top ten recipient countries in project counts and commitment value with $N > 50$ for the number of tweets were included in the analysis. We used the following query: (China OR Chinese) AND (AI OR Algorithms OR "Machine Learning" OR "Artificial Intelligence" OR "Surveillance" OR "Smart City" OR "Safe City" OR "CCTV" OR "Cloud Computing" OR "Data Center" OR "Remote Sensing" OR "Medical Imaging"). Brandwatch analysis is limited to English.

FIGURE 3.1

Percentages of Tweets That Showed Different Sentiments in Top China AI Recipient Countries, 2021–2022

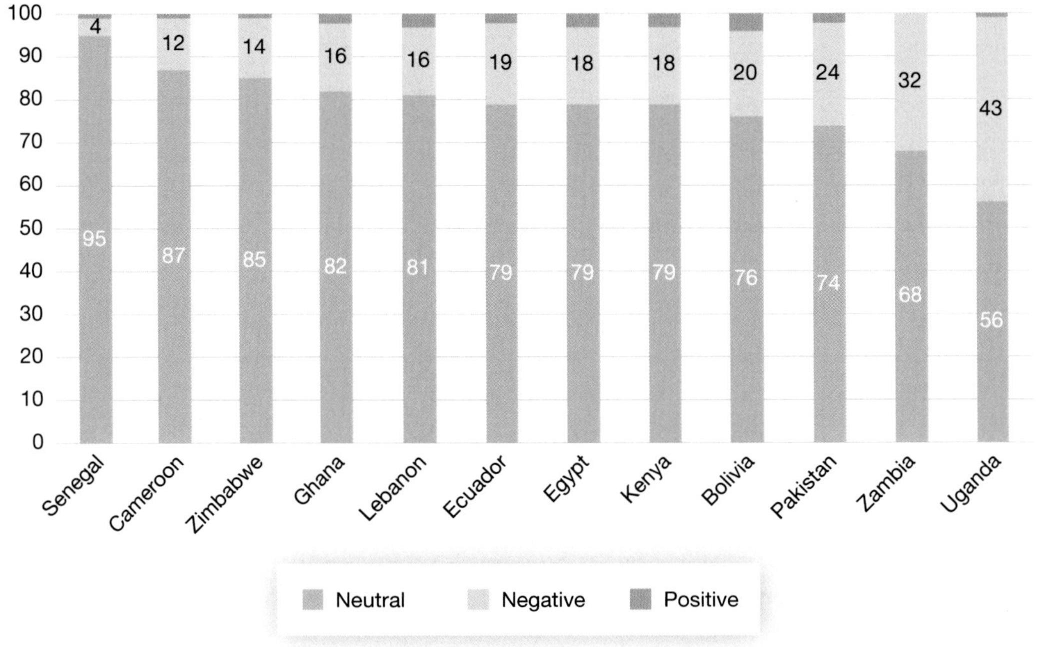

SOURCE: Authors' analysis of Twitter data using Brandwatch.

commitment in value and are English-speaking countries.[2] In addition, Kenya has emerged as an important center for AI technology in Africa because of its large pool of skilled tech talent and early adoption of AI services across multiple industries. Pakistan is one of the countries that has received major Chinese investment in Asia.[3] It also has significant potential to become an important center for AI technology because of its large population of young technical graduates and growing technology sector. These countries are further compelling as a pair of case studies because they are on different continents, and both are flawed democracies and have developing economies.

Each country's case study was based on in-depth stakeholder interviews. The findings from the two sources help us cross-validate and gain a less biased view on the rationales

---

[2] Compared with the average percentages of AI project counts (1.4 percent) and AI project commitment value (0.5 percent) among all projects in the GCDF 2.0 dataset, Pakistan and Kenya both have a slightly higher percentage of AI projects from China among all grants and loans received from China in terms of AI project counts (3.7 percent and 3.1 percent, respectively, compared with the average of 1.4 percent) and AI project commitment value (1.4 percent and 2.8 percent, respectively, compared with the average of 0.5 percent).

[3] Madiha Afzal, *"At All Costs": How Pakistan and China Control the Narrative on the China-Pakistan Economic Corridor*, Brookings Institution, June 2020.

FIGURE 3.2

Percentages of Tweets That Showed Different Emotions in Top China AI Recipient Countries, 2021–2022

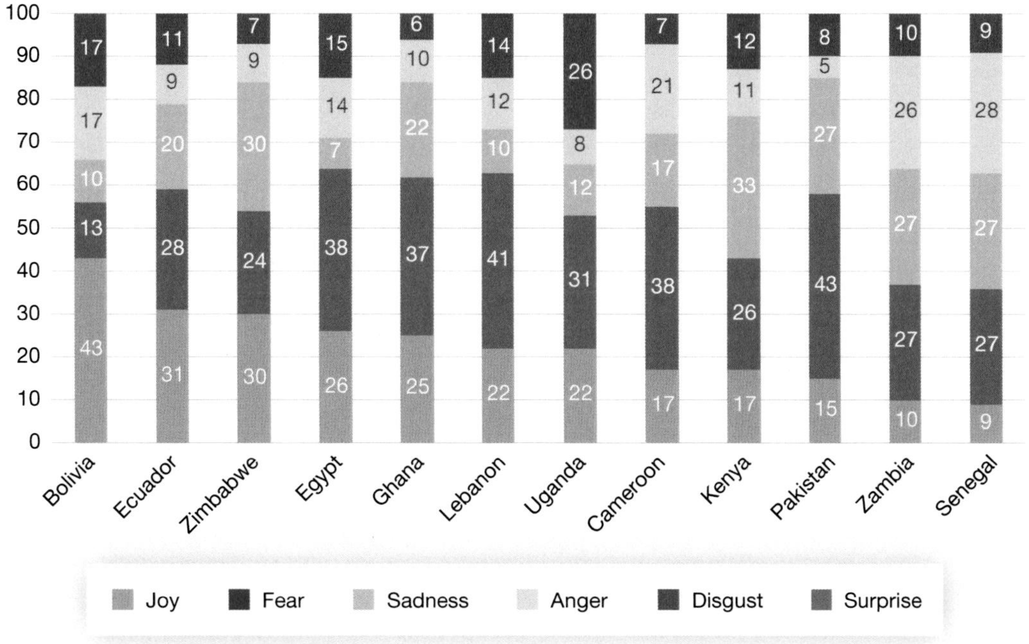

SOURCE: Authors' analysis of Twitter data using Brandwatch.

behind the impact of and perceptions toward China's AI technology exports. Detailed methodologies can be found in Appendix B.

Kenya

Kenya is considered a partly-free electoral autocracy, with growing wealth gaps, a lively civil society, and multiple data protection laws. China is a key trade partner for Kenya: The bilateral trade volume expanded from $471.6 million in 2007 to $2.88 billion a decade later. The two countries' governments have also had a longstanding diplomatic alliance. Chinese telecommunications firms have played a pivotal role in establishing significant digital infrastructure, such as the docking of submarine cables for the $425-million Pakistan and East Africa Connecting Europe cable.[4] This substantial project spans Asia and Africa and also includes France. Leveraging this robust infrastructure, the Kenyan government aims to establish

---

[4] Muriuki Mureithi and Judy Nyaguthii, *Telecommunication Ecosystem Evolution in Kenya, 2009–2019: Setting the Pace and Unbundling the Turbulent Journey to a Digital Economy in a 4IR Era*, Institute of Economic Affairs, 2021

high-speed connectivity and stimulate growth in the information and communication technology (ICT) sector. Notably, ZTE was responsible for laying the cables in the western regions of Kenya, while Huawei handled operations in Nairobi and the central parts of Kenya.

Empowered with this newly built capacity, the Kenyan government has initiated a variety of e-government projects, many of which rely on Chinese equipment and are financed by loans from the Export and Import Bank of China. Huawei was invited to install Kenya's Safe City project to improve public security. The first Safe City system by Huawei successfully connected 1,800 high-definition cameras and 200 high-definition traffic surveillance cameras across Nairobi. A command center was installed to support a police station with over 9,000 police officers.[5]

Other private Chinese companies have also actively participated in Kenya's technological transformation. For instance, in 2012, the Kenyan government awarded a tender to Nanjing Les Information Technology. This high-tech provider, known for offering urban traffic management tools and urban government solutions, was contracted to supply digital surveillance cameras. This collaboration signifies the continued engagement of China's private sector in the deployment and enhancement of Kenyan digital infrastructure.[6] The technical maintenance of the public security systems is also heavily reliant on Chinese contractors.

In 2023, the Pew Research Center examined Kenyan attitudes toward China and Chinese technology. When polled, Kenyans have a relatively positive view overall of China, although it has grown somewhat less positive recently. By a three-to-one ratio, Kenyans considered it beneficial to their country when China's economy was strong, and more Kenyans than not considered Chinese investment in Kenya to be good. Chinese technology is considered to be impressive and to provide strong data protections.[7]

People in Kenya have also started to notice the Chinese electronic and AI-enabled social media applications.[8] The little-known Transsion became the dominant player in Africa's mobile market, supported by users who cannot afford Apple, Samsung, or other smartphone brands.[9] Transsion's new phone, the Tecno Camon X Pro, has facial recognition technology, which will collect data from millions of customers. Chinese phone applications are also advanced in adapting to African skin tone preferences, and the Chinese Boomplay music

---

[5] Bulelani Jili, "Chinese Surveillance Tools in Africa, China, Law, and Development Project," University of Oxford, June 30, 2020.

[6] Bulelani Jili, "Africa's Demand for and Adoption of Chinese Surveillance Technology," Atlantic Council's Digital Forensic Research Lab, May 2023.

[7] Laura Silver, Christine Huang, and Laura Clancy, "China's Approach to Foreign Policy Gets Largely Negative Reviews in 24-Country Survey," Pew Research Center, July 27, 2023.

[8] Lynsey Chutel, "China Is Exporting Facial Recognition Software to Africa, Expanding Its Vast Database," Quartz, May 25, 2018.

[9] Abdullah, "Transsion: Q2 Brings Strong Growth for Africa's Leading Phone Seller," *Gizchina*, July 30, 2023.

application has a large African song bank.[10] At the same time, not all Chinese applications with AI technologies were successful in Kenya. For example, Tencent's attempt to enter the African market with its dominant WeChat application in 2013 encountered strong local competitors, and the company withdrew from the African market in 2017.[11]

Table 3.1 shows that three of the four AI application projects started between 2013 and 2017, and one Safe City or Smart City project was committed in 2012. There is one AI infrastructure project (on e-government), which was committed in 2007. These five AI projects account for 6 percent of the overall China AI export commitment value and 2.8 percent of the overall loans and grants received by Kenya (according to the GCDF 2.0 dataset). The five AI projects belong to the health (60 percent) and government and civil society (40 percent)

TABLE 3.1
Summary of China's AI Projects in Kenya, 2000–2017

Project Type	Technology Category	Sector	Amount (2017 USD, millions)	Commitment Year	Description
AI application	Medical imaging	Health	26.14	2014	Facilitated the acquisition of 20 pieces of magnetic resonance imaging equipment from Neusoft Medical Systems.
AI application	Medical imaging	Health	78.79	2017	Supplied computed tomography (CT) scanners for 37 public county hospitals.
AI application	Medical imaging	Health	10.69	2013	Constructed a modern medical wing with several units of medical equipment, including CT scanners and X-ray scanners, for Gatundu Level IV Hospital expansion.
AI application	Safe City or Smart City	Government and civil society	101.85	2012	Installed CCTV cameras in major cities and towns around the country.
AI infrastructure	E-government	Government and civil society	65.08	2007	Built a secure network for Kenyan e-government activities, called the Kenyan Government Unified Messaging System Project, to address disparities in technology that lead to less efficient electronic communication among Kenyan government officials.

SOURCE: Features information from CAIED.
NOTE: USD = U.S. dollars.

---

[10] Jenni March, "How China Is Slowly Expanding Its Power in Africa, One TV Set at a Time," CNN, July 24, 2019.

[11] Victor Ekwealor, "In Africa, OPay and WeChat Have More in Common Than Just Being Super Apps," Techpoint Africa, November 29, 2019.

sectors. Among 159 Chinese non-AI projects in Kenya between 2000 and 2017, many are in education (17.6 percent), transport and storage (13.2 percent), and government and civil society (13.2 percent).

What Factors Have Made China's AI Exports Competitive in Kenya?

According to interviewees from Kenya,[12] China is a dominant player in building digital infrastructure and providing AI tools in Africa. In addition, China has been the primary provider of cloud storage, data centers, and integrated AI-capable systems across Africa. Their "deal team packages" make the Chinese bidders competitive in public procurement:

> China was definitely the dominant player both at the level of offering cloud storage capabilities, building out data centers, and then integrating all of those technical systems with AI-capable tools and dominance. (Kenyan AI technology researcher)

According to the individuals we interviewed, Chinese AI exports provide several crucial features that set them apart from competitors. First, China's AI export projects offer a tailored and integrated package, which competitors do not:

> The Chinese do better in the public procurement of digital infrastructure because it comes with this deal team package . . . The officials from the [Export-Import Bank of China] would say that together we are going to work with you to prepare you to sell you a package. You won't need to pay any money right now . . . We'll cover everything, and that turnkey ability is what appeals to the African ministers . . . That's the magic formula for Huawei and the Smart City systems. (Journalist covering technology development in Africa)

Secondly, China's robust financing options provide a significant edge. China's Ministry of Commerce, the Bank of China, and two state-owned policy banks (the China Development Bank and the Export-Import Bank of China) offered 52 loans and export buyer's credits to AI application and AI infrastructure projects during the period from 2000 to 2017. One or more Chinese companies were included as contractors on the projects. These Chinese companies are able to offer equipment and services with the initial financial agreement; however, countries then have a dependence on these firms for ongoing maintenance, mandatory updates, and usage. This unique financing model is a major competitive advantage for Chinese firms, a point strongly underscored by the individuals we interviewed:

> The Chinese government has been subsidizing some initiatives . . . China, and specifically Huawei, sells their products at a cheaper rate that also comes with the loan. The reality is, to be able to compete with something that's cheaper, that also comes directly with the loan . . . If you are, for example, buying from Huawei, it doesn't come as a standalone tech-

---

[12] All interviews for Kenya were conducted from April 28, 2023, through May 24, 2023.

nology. It usually comes with the package. So, if you're buying surveillance cameras for your city, it also comes with the data center. It's comprehensive offerings of relatively good quality from a respected Chinese company. (Kenyan AI technology researcher)

Third, several interviewees pointed out that China's significant strides in AI technology can be attributed to its access to vast quantities of digital data from Africa through its long-term partnership with African countries. Additionally, many African leaders view China's approach—fostering economic growth while retaining social control—as an appealing model, and one that aligns well with their own national priorities.

One of the things that allows China to be the big power in artificial intelligence is access to digital data . . . which is the input that feeds AI and what is very attractive to many African leaders . . . is in the Chinese model . . . And so this mix of providing economic development while at the same time keeping control over societies and over populations has been very attractive to many African leaders. (Europe-based African technology researcher)

What Concerns Have Been Raised About Data Privacy and Data Usage?

Both recent interviews and the few projects documented in CAIED from 2000 to 2017 show that AI has not been widely used in government programs. However, limited uses of AI technology in the public sector have already raised some concerns among civil society about data safety and usage. Many interviewees expressed uncertainty about the specifics of data collection, as well as the ways in which these data have been and will continue to be used for AI applications. This lack of transparency regarding data acquisition and its intended use is particularly noticeable in government projects and programs. When discussing initiatives, such as the Kenyan National Integrated Identity Management System (Huduma Namba) and the Safe City projects in Nairobi, Kenyan interviewees displayed considerable ambiguity about the use of data:

There was one point in which biometric data was being collected by a French company [IDEMIA]. There was a court case and the ruling came down last year. They [IDEMIA] had to stop collecting biometric data because the government couldn't ensure that privacy protections would be upheld.[13] (U.S.-based Kenya AI technology researcher)

This is about what's up with that data, the digital ID, Huduma Namba. How are they used? How to even hold them accountable to that data? (a Kenyan AI specialist from a local nongovernmental organization [NGO])

---

[13] Frank Hersey, "NGOs Sue Idemia for Failing to Consider Human Rights Risks in Kenyan Digital ID," Biometric Update, July 29, 2022.

> We're not sure what that data [collected by CCTV cameras in Kenya] is used for. We do not feel like they [the government] actually protect the users, because if you are using my personal data to train the algorithms, how am I assured that what I'm giving you is protected? (Kenyan government staff in the Ministry of Information and Communication Technology)

Some interviewees also expressed concerns about the use of the data collected by the government. According to interviewees from that country, the Kenyan government has also employed AI technology to stifle political opposition, which is very concerning to some.

> We had something that we called Huduma Namba. So whereby someone is, your ID, your birth certificate, and everything were shown, but at the end of the day we ask ourselves, where will all that data [go] or where was all that data being used for? I remember . . . there was a scheme whereby people were being alerted to a scam . . . So apparently all that information was being siphoned from the database where the Huduma Namba was being stored, so you see that data can be used by fraudsters in a very bad way. (Kenyan AI specialist in media industry)

> I don't know how the police know to knock on our doors, but they know to knock on our doors after we send Facebook messages . . . The [Kenyan] government has been able to use Internet access to stifle opposition to halt communications and people see it and people know it . . . Political opposition and activists know that there is the capacity for surveillance if needed on social media. (U.S.-based African studies researcher)

Some of these concerns over data privacy and use stem from Kenyan citizens' lack of trust in government. Interviewees unanimously expressed low trust in their government, especially given how governments have used surveillance (non-AI) technologies against citizens in the past. Kenya is known for having a relatively vibrant and active civil society compared with many other countries in Africa, and the interviewees expressed strong suspicion of the Kenyan government:

> We tend not to trust our government so much. When the government is doing something, people look at it with a different attitude and different perspective. Maybe because of many things that have happened, anything that the government has implemented, it has tended to have a lot of controversy, including the new generation of the integrated national identity cards. (Kenyan AI specialist in business sector)

> I don't think the government is [trusted] in terms of data. What happened [to the national ID cards)]? Some other people never got those cards and millions of Kenyans went to those sessions to register for that . . . If we do not have a registered number, you wouldn't be able to access government funds. . . . Then they issued another one. What happened to the old one? They are using our data, maybe selling it to the highest bidder. (Kenyan AI specialist in media industry)

On the other hand, Kenyan interviewees expressed more trust in the AI technology used by the private sector. They seem to be quite comfortable sharing their data with private companies in exchange for access to convenient services, although they might not know what data are being collected. This might result from the limited harm and risks of sharing data with private sector companies, which cannot arrest people and are not as motivated to punish forms of activity that citizens see as legitimate or necessary:

> I think there's a difference between the [Kenyan] government sector and private sector with data collection—there's skepticism. When you have to go into a government office, you are required to share biodata . . . That technology is imposed on you, you have no power over how it will be used. With the private sector, I don't know if the average person knows what data is being collected on their phones . . . People may trust private [AI] technologies because data collection is less obvious. (U.S.-based African studies researcher)

> When it comes to the private sector [in Kenya], people feel that there's recourse in case things go wrong. You can hold somebody accountable. Government tends to be very amorphous. You don't know who will answer and who to hold accountable. (Kenyan AI specialist in the business sector)

Has the Promise of AI for Public Safety Been Realized?

More frustration with government use of AI manifested in the perception of the ineffectiveness of the AI technology implementation in Safe City or Smart City projects. Several interviewees mentioned that Safe City and Smart City projects have not improved the level of safety for the citizens as the government claimed it would.

> We don't get the feedback or the effect of the application of that technology [in Kenya]. They'll claim that the crime rate has reduced because CCTVs have been installed and maybe use things like facial recognition to detect and track criminals in the city. But we are not yet seeing the application of that. And we're not sure what that data is used for. (Kenyan government staff in the Ministry of ICT)

> The contract for the installation of security CCTV around the city of Nairobi was aimed at curbing the levels of crime in the city. . . . [But] sometimes things have happened, [but] we are not able to track because the system didn't capture. (Kenyan AI specialist in business sector)

One interviewee linked the lackluster performance of AI surveillance on crime reduction to lack of government resources, police training, and other governance systems:

> That's maybe too simple a solution because the expectation that a camera system is going to lead to a reduction in crime. The sociological reasons behind crime are very complex . . . but surveillance is part of an anti-crime package. The problem in many African countries, though, is that the governance underneath that is supposed to support the tech-

nology is weak. So there's police brutality issues. There's lack of resources, there's lack of training, so the cameras just don't really make the difference amid all the other challenges that they're facing. (Journalist covering technology development in Africa)

What Capacity Does the Kenyan Government Have in AI Policy and Technical Knowledge?

Another common theme in the interviews was how the Kenyan government lacked capacity to make full use of imported AI technologies. We identified three layers of governance capacities from the interviews.

Gaps in Data Protection Legislation, Data Governance, and Resources

Since November 25, 2019, the Data Protection Act, 2019 has been the main data protection law in Kenya. It carries out the provisions of Kenya's 2010 Constitution's, Article 31(c) and (d). The Data Protection (Civil Registration) Regulations, 2020 were announced in October 2020, and the Data Protection Commissioner was appointed on November 16, 2020.[14] Since that time, substantial work has gone into creating the rules that will govern how the Data Protection Act is put into practice, including three regulations, four guidelines,[15] and additional guidance.[16]

Although Kenya has some of the most established data protection laws among developing countries, most people we interviewed still see weaknesses in the legislation. Some interviewees were frustrated by the government's continued efforts to implement AI projects in the absence of a strong legal framework, despite civil society's efforts to promote data safety and slow down AI technology adoption:

> These interactions are problematic as [they raise] huge ethical concerns when it comes to the usage of AI, especially in projects tied to Smart Cities and Safe Cities. . . . But stringent data regulation policies aren't there [in Africa]. (Europe-based AI technology researcher)

> When many of these [AI] technologies arrive, they arrive usually either in weak legal arrangements or simply in legal spaces that are not necessarily well equipped to deal with the fallout consequences for them. The civil society has been spending a good amount of time really trying to either advocate the bolstering of these capabilities or try to curb the spell out consequences for surveillance. There's been great attention simply at trying to sometimes even slow down the state's adoption of [AI] systems. . . . It's the gap between

---

[14] DLA Piper, "Kenya," webpage, January 12, 2023.

[15] Guidance Note on Registration of Data Controllers and Data Processors, Guidance Note on Processing Personal Data for Electoral Purposes, Guidance Note on Data Protection Impact Assessment, Guidance Note on Consent (DLA Piper, 2023).

[16] Complaints Management Manual, Alternative Disputes Resolution Framework (DLA Piper, 2023).

the speed of adoption of systems and the weakness of legal arrangements [in Kenya] that exacerbates civil liberties and challenges. (Kenyan AI technology researcher)

In addition, when asked about the data protection legislation on AI technology in their country, interviewees emphasized the overall lack of data governance, including limited capacity for regulation and law enforcement:

> That seems to me that the major issue [for Kenya] would be the governance issue . . . there is no supporting structure, no data protection law, no institutional capacity . . . They don't have the infrastructure of law and they don't have the ability to execute. And even if they did . . . they don't have the enforcement . . . They don't know how to regulate it because it's not indigenous. It's a foreign governance structure that's imposed on a political system that is far more dynamic and multifaceted than a Geneva written code governance structure. (Journalist covering technology development in Africa)

On the other hand, some interviewees were against government spending on AI and data technology, considering these activities could take up resources that should be used in delivering basic services to citizens.

> This is a systemic issue for them [the Kenyan government] beyond that. Tech is not the top priority for them. Delivering basic services is the top priority. (Journalist covering technology development in Africa)

Gaps in Local Technology Capacity

According to the interviewees, the vast majority of government officials are not knowledgeable about AI, and there are too few AI specialists who are aware of the power and potential dangers of applying AI technologies. Interviewees also mentioned that the public sector lags well behind both the local private sector and the public sector in other developed nations in terms of technology capacity:

> It's a good initiative [public sector AI projects in Kenya] because I've seen other countries embrace the same technology and they have seen and reached the benefit. It's a promising technology . . . but we are not yet there to fully embrace this new technology. (Europe-based African technology researcher)

The lack of technical capacity in the country makes it unable to maintain the complex AI projects and sustain the technological transfer from these imported Chinese AI projects, which also increases the risks of data security.

> You have these sophisticated AI algorithms that are controlled often by Chinese firms . . . Local African firms often don't have the technical capacity to mobilize AI, so they rely on their Chinese counterparts to come up with the algorithms and the software that enable them to exploit this data. (Europe-based African technology researcher)

> African countries are still very much technically dependent on China [to] produce the technology and having the local expertise to maintain the given projects remains a general and continuing struggle on the continent. (Kenyan AI technology researcher)

Some interviewees also identified local language as a barrier to AI technology transfer because of the lack of interoperability in software and systems:

> The biggest bottleneck of adopting Chinese technologies on the software, particularly for a country like Kenya, is language . . . We don't understand Chinese when we integrate in other things . . . So that's why we have a lot of our services coming from the American companies. (Kenyan AI specialist in intergovernmental educational institute)

Pakistan

China and Pakistan share a longstanding relationship that has its roots in various historical, political, and socioeconomic connections since the early 1960s. In the past decade, the bilateral relationship escalated with a new economic dimension.[17] The China-Pakistan Economic Corridor (CPEC), a flagship project under China's BRI, is a $62 billion 10-year project aimed to connect Gwadar Port in southwestern Pakistan with China's northwestern region, facilitating a new major energy corridor, along with development for economic growth and trade.[18] In addition to CPEC, both nations have concurred to intensify their technological collaboration with the BRI platform.[19] This alignment is in sync with the trajectory of BRI's evolution into the Digital Silk Road, which emphasizes the expansion of ICT infrastructure, digital services, e-commerce, and the establishment of smart cities.

Efforts to digitize government processes in Pakistan predated CPEC. For example, an initiative—the National Database and Registration Authority (NADRA), under the Ministry of Interior—was established in 1998 to introduce universal digital identifiers for all Pakistanis.[20] In recent years, efforts have been made to introduce online taxation and utility payment systems, digital land records, and public complaint resolution platforms.[21] Professionals in Pakistan see AI as being important to understand: In one 2022 study, more than 80 percent of Pakistani doctors and medical students were unfamiliar with medical applications of AI,

---

[17] Manjari Chatterjee Miller, "How China and Pakistan Forged Close Ties," Council on Foreign Relations, October 3, 2022.

[18] Syed Fazl-E-Haider, "China's Big Gamble in Pakistan: A 10-Year Scorecard for CPEC," *The Interpreter*, August 1, 2023.

[19] Sana Jamal, "Pakistan, China Urged to Boost Tech Cooperation," *Gulf News*, July 20, 2022.

[20] Devex, "National Database and Registration Authority (NADRA)," webpage, undated.

[21] Zafar Bhutta, "Govt to Use NADRA's Database to Detect Tax Evaders," *Express Tribune*, March 13, 2019.

but more than 75 percent supported the inclusion of AI in medical training.[22] However, the transition to e-government also presents challenges. The digital divide, cybersecurity threats, and the need for digital literacy are all significant concerns that need to be addressed to maximize the potential benefits of e-government.

In recent months, Pakistan has been engulfed in a political crisis triggered by the April 2022 parliamentary vote that ousted the government of former Prime Minister Imran Khan. Following attacks on military installations on May 9, 2023, in response to Khan's arrest, thousands of political activists have been detained, and robust controls have been established on electronic media.[23] Pakistan is currently also entrenched in severe economic distress with increasing external debt, now amounting to $100 billion, a third of which is owed to China. In the summer of 2023, Pakistan narrowly averted a default on its foreign debt through a strenuous eight-month negotiation that culminated in a $3 billion deal with the International Monetary Fund. The country's economic crisis is exacerbating the living conditions of its citizens: Inflation has risen to 29.4 percent; food and transport costs are up by 40 percent and 20 percent, respectively; and poverty rates are projected to reach 37.2 percent.[24] The high prices of electricity and fuel hinder the masses from reaping the benefits of CPEC's additional energy and improved highways.

Pakistan is also considered a partly free electoral autocracy with limited data protection legislation. The country received nine AI projects from China between 2000 and 2017. As Table 3.2 shows, Pakistan has five AI application projects: one education project that was committed in 2007, one Safe City or Smart City project that was committed in 2010, and three government and civil society projects that were committed between 2011 and 2014. The government and civil society projects are three separate grants provided by the Chinese government to the Government of Pakistan for the "9.26" military defense project that involved the acquisition of unmanned aerial vehicles (UAVs). These three projects amounted to a total of over $50 million (constant 2017 U.S. dollars). Between 2009 and 2017, Pakistan also received four AI infrastructure projects, consisting of one Safe City or Smart City project and three remote sensing and seismic monitoring projects. Two of the remote sensing and seismic monitoring projects were loans committed by the Export-Import Bank of China for the Paksat-1R Project, which involved construction of a DFH-4-type satellite by the Pakistan Space and

---

[22] Zaboor Ahmed, Khurram Khaliq Bhinder, Amna Tariq, Muhammad Junaid Tahir, Qasim Mehmood, Muhammad Saad Tabassum, Muna Malik, Sana Aslam, Muhammad Sohaib Asghar, and Zohaib Yousaf, "Knowledge, Attitude, and Practice of Artificial Intelligence Among Doctors and Medical Students in Pakistan: A Cross-Sectional Online Survey," *Annals of Medicine and Surgery*, Vo. 76, 2022.

[23] Human Rights Watch, "Pakistan: Mass Arrests Target Political Opposition," May 20, 2023.

[24] Fazl-E-Haider, 2023

TABLE 3.2

Summary of China's AI Projects in Pakistan, 2000–2017

Project Type	Technology Category	Sector	Amount (2017 USD, millions)	Commitment Year	Description
AI application	Safe City or Smart City	Government and civil society	151.77	2010	The Islamabad Safe City project implemented by Huawei Technologies in coordination with Pakistan's NADRA, which supported the installation of 1,950 surveillance CCTV cameras in Islamabad
AI application	Unmanned vehicles	Government and civil society	16.52	2011	A military project that the Government of Pakistan's Economic Affairs Division refers to as "9.26," a codename for a defense project that involves the acquisition of UAVs
AI application	Unmanned vehicles	Government and civil society	20.99	2012	Additional Chinese government grants for the 9.26 project
AI application	Unmanned vehicles	Government and civil society	12.51	2014	Additional Chinese government grants for the 9.26 project
AI application	Other	Education	5.47	2007	The establishment of the Precision Mechanical and Technology Centre at the Pakistan Council of Scientific and Industrial Research in Lahore. The center is equipped with state-of-the-art equipment, such as computer numerical control (CNC) lathe machines, CNC milling machines, and three-dimensional arm scanners
AI infrastructure	Safe City or Smart City	Government and civil society	4.41	2016	The development of Gwadar Smart Port City Master Plan is intended to transform the existing city into a modern port of international standards and a smart, sustainable city that can drive local, national, and regional growth in the coming decades

Table 3.2—Continued

Project Type	Technology Category	Sector	Amount (2017 USD, millions)	Commitment Year	Description
AI infrastructure	Remote sensing and seismic monitoring	Communications	153.00	2017	A remote sensing satellite system project that will operate at an altitude of 640 kilometers and will enable Pakistan to meet its imagery requirements in the areas of land mapping, agriculture classification and assessment, urban and rural planning, environmental monitoring, natural disaster management, and water resource management for socioeconomic development
AI infrastructure	Remote sensing and seismic monitoring	Communications	152.67	2009	Paksat-1R, a DFH-4-type satellite launched on the Long March 3B rocket, with a design life of 15 years and initial goals to provide broadband internet access, digital television broadcasting, remote and rural telephony, emergency communications, tele-education, and telemedicine services across South and Central Asia, Eastern Europe, East Africa and the Far East
AI infrastructure	Remote sensing and seismic monitoring	Communications	15.44	2010	Additional Chinese government loans for the Paksat-1R satellite project

SOURCE: Features information from CAIED.

Upper Atmosphere Research Commission and the China Great Wall Industry Corporation, and the accompanying construction of a ground control facility. The third remote sensing project was a governmental concessional loan in 2017 for Pakistan's Remote Sensing Satellite System project. These three projects amounted to a total of over $321 million (constant 2017 U.S. dollars). These nine AI application and AI infrastructure projects make up 12 percent of China's total AI export commitment value in these years and 1.4 percent of all loans and grants that Pakistan has ever received (according to AidData's GCDF 2.0 dataset).

Whereas the top sectors of the AI projects are communications (44.4 percent) and government and civil society (33.3 percent), including defense (Table 3.2), the top sectors of the 235 non-AI projects are emergency response (32.8 percent), energy (17.5 percent), and transport and storage (12.8 percent).

What Factors Have Made China's AI Exports Competitive in Pakistan?

Interviewees from Pakistan echoed similar issues to the issues brought up in Kenya.[25] Respondents noted that Chinese technology vendors offer more cost-effective and budget-friendly solutions for developing countries, such as Pakistan, as compared with the alternatives. Moreover, the Chinese government demonstrate flexibility in working within the limitations and constraints faced by countries with fewer resources. These competitive advantages in terms of affordable pricing and flexibility have led developing countries, such as Pakistan, to become reliant on Chinese technologies rather than to explore more expensive and inflexible alternatives:

> Their technologies and solutions are more cost-effective. So, if you are a developing country and you have a limited budget, then they are more flexible to work with you as a vendor for hardware and software solutions and everything like that. (Pakistani AI entrepreneur and professor)

> Pakistan is not only dependent upon Chinese government technology. They are not even exploring the technologies available in Europe, Germany . . . I think because it's easier to access Chinese technologies and it's comparatively cheaper. (Pakistani AI entrepreneur and former staff of NADRA)

What Concerns Have Been Raised About Data Privacy and Data Usage?

In Pakistan, there is still little application of AI in the public sector, according to the findings of stakeholder interviews and the descriptive statistics reported in Chapter 2. As one interviewee noted,

> In terms of the public sector [in Pakistan] at large, the AI footprint is very, very small. . . . I think healthcare [in Pakistan] is an example [of AI technology application in the public sector]. Imaging and diagnostics using AI for early detection can lead to more accurate detection. . . . [We can also use] feeds from rural and distant communities to pass on all that data. However, we're very far away from these kinds of mainstream applications for public service delivery . . . the whole concept of AI assistance helping citizens access public services and digitized public services is very far away. (Pakistani AI technology researcher)

However, as in Kenya, these restricted applications of AI technology in the public sphere have already sparked some worries in civil society about the security and use of data. A recurring topic in the interviews was that the participants were mostly unaware of the data that

---

[25] All interviews for Pakistan were conducted from May 16, 2023, through June 6, 2023.

had been gathered and how it had been and would be used for AI purposes. This lack of transparency about data collection and use was particularly pervasive for government projects and activities. Interviewees from Pakistan often raised questions about data usage and storage, especially when discussing the NADRA, the Pakistan national ID system, and the Safe City projects.

> Everything [about NADRA] is biometrically verified and enabled. . . . There are a lot of question marks on how that has been used and how the privacy and protection of data is in place. . . . There was very little transparency around it [the Safe City project in Islamabad], and on what kind of technology was deployed inside Pakistan and its integration with NADRA and other agencies. (Pakistani AI entrepreneur and former staff of NADRA)

> There was a major leak of our data. But there is no concrete thing which has happened around that . . . Where is the cloud, where is Pakistan's cloud? Where are we putting this data? Where is that data center? (Pakistani ICT researcher)

Most interviewees in Pakistan specifically expressed concern about the potentially harmful use of AI technologies, although they also mentioned that most Pakistan citizens might not share the same concerns. Interviewees commented on how AI technologies could be used by law enforcement agencies unlawfully to track civil movements and suppress social protests:

> AI could have done so much more—it could have strengthened the democracy [in Pakistan] in so many ways . . . [but] we are using that AI technology or the safety cameras for catching those people who are protesting for their rights . . . really a shame what we are doing with those cameras. We are not using it properly. (Pakistani ICT researcher)

These concerns were replicated in our analysis of Twitter data. Pakistani users, whether talking about the United States or China, were more likely to reference military use of AI relative to a normal text sample.

Like what was observed in Kenya, Pakistanis' lack of trust in their government might be a contributing factor to their concerns about data privacy and usage. Some respondents said they had little trust in their government, especially considering how the government had previously employed surveillance (non-AI) technologies against protestors. Respondents also specifically mentioned the lack of trust they have in government law enforcement agencies, largely because of these agencies' recent track record of using heavy-handed tactics against civil society. However, it is important to point out that our sample might not represent the majority view of all citizens in the country, and the distrust might have been there for many years, and using AI merely supports that feeling of mistrust:

> These laws or policies [in Pakistan] would not matter at all . . . Say something else and the authorities are exactly opposite to that, and they get away with it . . . And then nobody bothers about it as well until unless it hits them . . . Over the years we have seen only the opposite of what I love would require [the Pakistan government] to do so. So that situation

will continue . . . Unless they have the control on everything, [the public sector AI projects are] not going to work. (Pakistani AI specialist in local NGO)

Has the Promise of AI for Public Safety Been Realized?

Some interviewees from Pakistan expressed concerns over Safe City and Smart City projects and questioned the actual impact and purpose of this AI technology use:

> I have not seen anyone [in Pakistan] getting any benefit from this Safe City or people feeling a bit safer after the Safe City . . . We have ample evidence that it had not helped in any way . . . If we see these safety cameras from Karachi to Gawadar and Gawadar to Punjab, it's all about surveillance, face recognition, and citizen movements. There is no legal framework and no privacy, so it's data security centric surveillance . . . So that's why I think AI is not serving the public, but instead it's capturing the rights of the people in terms of privacy rights [given] there is no privacy law in Pakistan. (Pakistani AI specialist in local NGO)

Interviewees who were involved with safety projects while working at NADRA also mentioned how technical and organizational barriers prevented them from performing predictive analytics and greater functionality of the Safe City projects.

> We had developed different software to automate policing, which includes criminal record office . . . We automated that and what we did is then we had started some predictive analysis . . . We can't integrate with our existing criminal record office or vehicle system, which is record of theft vehicles . . . So we can't get it integrated till now. For the upcoming [Safe City] projects of the three cities, after learning this lesson, what we did is we are just preparing hardware in camera and we are trying to develop our own software . . . Once it is done, then other databases will be integrated with this technology and then we might be able to start predictive analysis and some other things like this. So, I guess at this point of time, we are far behind and maybe in another year or two we will be able to start some predictive analysis on these safety projects. (Pakistani government official in Punjab Information Technology Board)

What Capacity Does the Pakistani Government Have in AI Policy and Technical Knowledge?

Another recurring theme from the interviews was how Pakistan's limitations as a country hindered it from using imported AI technologies to their full potential. Below, we briefly explain the limitations and gaps that were highlighted in the study.

Gaps in Data Protection Legislation and Data Governance

Like Kenya, Pakistan has some existing data protection legislation. The Constitution of 1973 states that "the privacy of home, shall be inviolable," and courts have interpreted that to be a generalized privacy requirement. However, that same passage is preceded by a very different clause: "and subject to law."[26] This has left sufficient holes, and respondents agreed that there was no meaningful, consistent national regulation. That does not mean that no such regulation exists. Punjab, for example, has a strong and effective privacy law.[27] The Prevention of Electronic Crimes Act, 2016 already accomplishes some of the same goals. Additionally, the Ministry of Information Technology and Telecommunications has introduced a consultation draft of the Personal Data Protection Bill 2021 with the intention of having it become law following public comment, approval from both Houses of Parliament, and receipt of assent from the President of Pakistan.[28]

However, most interviewees pointed out the inadequate data protection laws in Pakistan despite the existing legislation. When asked about their country's data protection laws relating to AI technology, interviewees emphasized the general lack of data governance, particularly the absence of capacity for regulation and law enforcement:

> [Pakistan has] really bad data regimes in the public sector . . . the data policy is fragmented across different departments and tiers. All devolved subjects and the data fall under the provincial and the local domains, so coming up with the data policy is not going to be enough . . . I don't think people have thought about data in a way that would benefit the deployment of AI for the kind of scale we could leverage it for . . . We do need a revamp of data regimes across the board. (Pakistani AI technology researcher)

Gaps in Local Technology Capacity

As in Kenya, interviewees in Pakistan indicated that there are not enough AI specialists who are aware of the possible benefits and risks of applying AI technologies and that the vast majority of government officials are ignorant of the field. In terms of technology capacity, interviewees also said that the public sector lags far behind both the local private sector and the public sector in other developed countries:

> [Pakistan is] just not ready institutionally country-wise at any level to really secure the systems and really understand the negative side of AI and have all the right educational framework and degrees in place which can tell our developers and our AI experts what are the social and ethical constraints and biases in the data . . . My biggest worry as an indi-

---

[26] The Constitution of the Islamic Republic of Pakistan, "Part II: Fundamental Rights and Principles of Policy," webpage, undated.

[27] Punjab Safe Cities Authority, *Data and Privacy Protection Procedures (DP3)*, undated.

[28] United Nations Conference on Trade and Development, 2021; DLA Piper, undated.

vidual is that our lack of understanding of AI, of ethics, and of its complete impact on the society. That's a big problem right now. (Pakistani AI technology researcher)

I think it's a bit early on for [public sector AI projects in Pakistan] because at this point of time, we are sitting far behind the stage. We can't really analyze what AI is as a government because we are just developing different systems at the moment. (Pakistani government official in Punjab Information Technology Board)

The country's technological incapacity prevents it from being able to capture and sustain the technological transfer from the imported China AI projects and complicated AI projects:

We have seen some local companies were hired to develop [AI] mechanisms to run on these infrastructure . . . But at the lower hierarchy level, not in the upper hierarchy. The same also happened when they were installing the cable . . . The technical labor was hired from Pakistan, but all implementation was done by Chinese themselves. (Pakistani AI specialist in local NGO)

In summary, the country case study provided an in-depth analysis of sentiments on China's AI in Kenya and Pakistan, two recipient countries with AI projects. Although they reflected the advantage that China has on AI markets, the interviewees and social media analysis also suggested the public's deep concerns about data safety, about the motivations for AI-aided surveillance or service registry, about the government's AI literacy, and about the dependency on imported technology in critical sectors. The limited ability of the recipient country to absorb the AI technology, on the other hand, can slow down the AI threats imposed on society.

CHAPTER 4

Implications of the Key Findings

In this chapter, we answer the key research questions by summarizing both the quantitative and qualitative data presented in the previous chapters.

How Have the AI Exports Financed by the Chinese Government Evolved Between 2000 and 2017?

Between 2000 and 2017, China's AI exports showed significant growth (Figure 2.1). Over this period, China's development-financed AI exports escalated, increasing by three- to four-fold from 2005 to 2012. Following this ascent, the numbers remained relatively stable after 2012, indicating a sustained plateau in growth. The slower growth observed after 2012 can be attributed to the fact that growth was increasingly driven by AI applications rather than infrastructure, whereby the Chinese *public* development-funded AI applications projects became less competitive against other competitors compared with the advantages enjoyed by the AI infrastructure projects.

The increase in AI export volume and corresponding funding is linked to the surge in AI infrastructure projects initiated after 2005 (Figure 2.1). These projects included key infrastructure, such as data centers, optic fiber networks, exports of surveillance camera systems, and training, among others. These AI infrastructure projects also tend to carry a higher cost than AI exports. Despite the significant investments made in both types of AI projects, the investments represented a relatively minor fraction of China's total overseas development financing activities: The combined financial commitment to AI endeavors amounted to a modest 1 to 3 percent of China's overall overseas development financed activities by 2017.

What Factors Have Made China's AI Exports Competitive in the Developing World?

A key factor underlying China's competitiveness in AI is its *integrated approach* to technology exports. China's public-financed projects provide not only AI technology applications and financing options but also the AI infrastructure projects that lay the foundation for these technologies in developing nations, such as the construction of data centers, laying of fiber optic cables, and installation of surveillance cameras and hardware. Subject-matter experts have also pointed out that Chinese negotiators sometimes offer loan packages or gifts related to other projects during negotiations. Although such package deals can enhance the success rate of the negotiations, they can also intensify perceptions of opaque or "murky" transactions.

Another key factor is the *affordability* of Chinese AI products. Chinese private companies' success in producing some of the most popular electronics has built up China's soft power on technology in these countries, aiding in the successful integration and acceptance of AI exports. Items, such as handsets and gaming gear, are attractively priced, which appeals significantly to the younger generation in these countries. This cost-effectiveness opens the door to technology for a larger demographic, reinforcing China's market presence in these regions.

In addition, China exhibits a high degree of *flexibility* in its operations. Its projects are often tailored to the recipient countries' requirements, providing additional financial packages and modifying timelines as needed. This adaptability fosters stronger relationships and contributes to the success of Chinese AI exports.

Such flexibility is partly rooted in China's strategic long-term focus, which includes a willingness to *engage with fragile political environments and a disregard for regime types*, broadening potential markets' scope. China is ready to engage with politically unstable or economically uncertain countries, unlike other AI providers. Furthermore, China's AI initiative emphasizes long-term soft power, a departure from the conventional corporation model that seeks quick profits for stakeholders. This approach fosters a higher willingness for technology application transfers, demonstrating a commitment to mutual benefit and long-term collaboration. China's unique blend of risk-taking, political neutrality, and strategic vision has boosted the global popularity and influence of its AI exports.

Which Countries, Industry Sectors, and Social Domains Have Been Most Affected by China's AI Exports?

We found that China's development-financed AI exports have enabled the growth of a significant AI application presence in host countries and provided venues for Chinese exporters. AI technologies related to medical imaging, Safe City or Smart City, and e-government have dominated AI use in the health, government, and communication sectors. In the latter part of this period (2000–2017), remote sensing technology also emerged as a new focus for AI applications, a trend in line with the overall evolution of AI technology in the past two decades.

A closer look at the geographic distribution of China's AI exports during this period reveals a wide spectrum of recipient countries, predominantly China's BRI partner countries. These include developing nations across Asia, Africa, and Latin America. Because most developing countries are autocracies, it is not a surprise that our analysis indicated that most of the countries that imported AI projects of different sectors were not liberal democracies (given that most LMIC are not in this category) but fall under non-liberal democratic categories: electoral democracy (31.0 to 46.0 percent), electoral autocracy (46.6 to 58.1 percent), or closed autocracy (7.0 to 9.3 percent) (Figure 2.5 and 2.6).

Interestingly, when we compared the allocation of AI projects to non-AI contracts, we found no particular bias toward any specific political regime within these three categories. Moreover, in closed autocracies, the application of AI in the government sector was less prevalent than it was in the health and communications sectors. More surprisingly, AI projects were more commonly found in countries that are classified by Freedom House as *free countries* than were non-AI projects.

Our finding is consistent with studies that suggest that politicians in free and electoral-governance nations with lower or middle incomes frequently seek out China's AI projects as a demonstration of their political performance.[1] In such scenarios, leaders facing electoral pressure might find China's AI application and AI infrastructure technologies particularly attractive, given the comprehensive packages that China offers for building safe and smart cities, which in turn underscores the government's commitment to reducing crime and enhancing government efficiency. However, we later also see feedback from the public on the disappointment in the failing of AI projects to reduce crime rates as promised by their government.

Finally, we also noticed that the nations with strict and robust data protection laws were more likely to have AI projects, particularly AI technologies pertaining to the government and communication sectors. However, we also noted that people are concerned about the effectiveness of law enforcement and that many of the countries receiving China's overseas finance are still in the process of formulating their data protection policies, and the robustness of these legislative initiatives remains in question. This is not a surprising discovery because regulations often lag behind the technology frontier; however, this adds to the question as to whether China's advanced AI regulations and its unique focus on whole society conformity on politics will influence the recipient countries' policy making.[2]

How Does the Public in the Recipient Countries View China's AI Exports?

Our in-country interviews and social media analysis showed that the perception of China's AI exports is multifaceted, differing considerably between the upper administration of the government and the public in recipient countries. A close look at these dynamics paints an intriguing picture of how China's technology and financial offerings are both embraced and viewed with skepticism.

---

[1] Jili, 2023.

[2] Sheehan, 2023.

On the one hand, top administrators in developing countries often favor China's AI exports, viewing them as well-suited to their national needs. Several factors contribute to this favorable perception. First, China assists in the development of comprehensive technology ecosystems, an initiative that appeals to countries that are looking to enhance their technological infrastructure. In addition, China provides funding for these infrastructure projects, easing the financial burden on these developing nations. Lastly, China's approach to project customization caters to the unique political needs of recipient countries, an aspect of China's strategy that is widely appreciated.

Despite this positive perception at the administrative level, the public's sentiment toward AI exports generally tends to be more negative. This unfavorable outlook can be traced back to concerns over the lack of transparency on project procurement processes, concerns over their governments' lack of capability for effectively using AI technologies, and worries over data privacy and safety. The apprehension stems from a perceived mismatch between their governments' motivation to adopt AI and a potential lack of technical competency or preparedness to handle the associated challenges.

An additional cause for dissatisfaction lies in the perceived inefficiency of AI in crime reduction within "safe cities." Despite the promises of using advanced AI technology to improve security, the public often perceives that tangible results are lacking. This disparity between expectations and outcomes further exacerbates public skepticism and fuels discontent among members of the public. It also caused some sectors in the public to wonder if the real motivation of the Safe City initiative was to conduct public surveillance for political gain rather than for crime reduction.

Limitations

As a pioneering research endeavor on a critical technology policy subject, our study inevitably encountered a series of challenges, described below.

Quantitative Study

One of the primary constraints was timing and data availability. Our research relied heavily on AidData data that were available before the project ends in September 2023. The data we use span the years 2000 to 2017 and is one of the few datasets equipped with comprehensive documentation of China's overseas development financing activities. This period precedes China's formulation of its major AI development policy and regulations, potentially limiting the scope of our quantitative analysis regarding China's latest strategic AI export endeavors and mismatching with our qualitative data analysis that uses more-recent opinion data. It also overlaps with the peak of investment activity in China's BRI between 2013 and 2017, which might bias the finding about China's heavy investment in the latter part of the study period. **Our research team will update the report when the 2018–2021 data becomes available in winter 2023.**

We also wrestled with the issue of disparate definitions of AI. Given the vastness of the AI field, definitions can differ greatly depending on such factors as technical complexity, functionality, and areas of application. The lack of a universally recognized definition of AI might have affected our analysis and the subsequent findings.

One potentially important aspect of China's AI that we did not explore using the dataset is the convention of *gifting* as part of China's grant or loan packages. Whereas the United States cracks down fairly strictly on corruption via the Foreign Corrupt Practices Act, which is known to reduce investment by U.S. companies in relatively corrupt countries (Graham and Stroup, 2016), Chinese companies and government agencies presumably perceive as mere "politeness" official gifts made to legislators, such as 15 luxury cars for Cote d'Ivoire, 20 sedans to Samoa, three concierge cars to Kenya's foreign ministry, six concierge cars for Micronesia's foreign ministry, two luxury vehicles for a victory day parade in Belarus, 50 luxury cars for the Republic of Guinea, and 50 saloon cars for the Sudanese president's office,[3] among other gifts identified.[4] In this project, we did not have enough information to examine the role of gifting as part of the AI exports from China.

Finally, we incorporated multiple indices in our research, specifically the V-Dem Democracy Index, the Electoral Democracy Index, United Nations Data Protection Law Status, DLA Piper Index, and the Technology Sector Index.[5] Although these indices enrich our analysis by providing diverse perspectives, it is important to note that each index carries its own limitations. Their different methodological approaches, inherent biases, and scope limitations might have subtly influenced our study's outcomes. Nonetheless, our research represents an important first step in understanding the nuances of China's AI exports and their global implications.

Interviews for Country Case Study

During the interviews, we noted the lack of transparency and uncertainty about a consistent definition of AI technology and its applications. Except for a few technicians and professionals that were currently using specific AI algorithms, most interviewees expressed confusion over the definition of AI technology, especially at the application level. The lack of shared understanding of AI technology might result from the fact that AI is a broad, complex, and rapidly evolving interdisciplinary field that encompasses diverse technologies, theories, and applications, leading to varied perspectives and definitions depending on one's viewpoint and background. The small number of in-country interviews ($N = 18$) (because of limited funding) also cast questions on the representativeness of the findings. The fact that RAND is U.S.-based and conducts interviews on this sensitive topic caused many government officials,

---

[3] AidData, "Global Chinese Development Finance," webpage, undated, Project IDs 66145, 49662, 60163, 63751, 66830, 2369, and 30422.

[4] Custer et al., 2021; Dreher et al., 2022.

[5] Bouey et al., 2023b.

especially in Pakistan, to decline comments. On the other hand, we were successful in finding in-country collaborators to help reach out to subject-matter experts in academia, think tanks, business communities, and civil societies. We also hired in-country researchers to conduct the interviews to reduce cultural barriers and interview bias.

Social Media Analysis

There are several caveats to our Brandwatch interpretations of Twitter data. First, we only examined social media posts, and social media is well-known as a limited source that introduces selection bias that skews toward urban, younger, and wealthier.[6] Also, social media analysis only allows us to observe and analyze posts; it cannot explain users' intentions and mental states.

While acknowledging these caveats, there is value in this kind of social media monitoring to better understand public opinion. Social media is a rich data source that has great research potential to detect subtle worries about future outcomes and addresses the scalability challenges presented by labor-intensive interviews. Methods like these present a unique opportunity to leverage analytical capabilities, especially in an age of AI.

---

[6] For example, see Dhiraj Murthy, Alexander Gross, Alexander Pensavalle, "Urban Social Media Demographics: An Exploration of Twitter Use in Major American Cities," *Journal of Computer-Mediated Communication*, Vol. 21, No. 1, January 1, 2016.

CHAPTER 5

Policy Recommendations

In an interconnected world facing unprecedented technological advancements, development aid that incorporates transformative AI applications holds the potential to transform governments, economies, and societies. When applied successfully, such aid programs can empower nations to tackle critical issues, such as crime reduction, social service delivery, health care efficiency, and economic development. However, AI applications in government and communications also have risks, including increasing repression and instability.

Our study aimed to understand how China's AI exports have been distributed in recent years and to obtain critical feedback from the recipients of these exports. The results of stakeholder interviews and the descriptive statistics reveal that there is still little use of AI in the public sector of recipient countries, although the upward trajectory over time is clear. But even the limited use of AI technology in the public sector has already demonstrated some negative impacts on civil society. The lack of transparency in AI project procurement, inadequate data governance policies or implementation, and the limited technological capability of many recipient countries means that countries that have invested significant funding and loans in AI technology for e-governance still face a paradox: Using AI technology to solve social problems in the public sector might exacerbate these issues and cause more severe harm to the populace as a whole.

To maximize the positive impact of development assistance that uses AI technology and to reduce waste, fraud, and risks, we draw from our analysis of China's AI exports from 2000 to 2017 to make the following recommendations for donors and recipient countries (and, in one case, investors) as priorities on AI technology imports and exports.

Recommendations

Recommendation 1: Policymakers should ensure openness and accountability concerning AI imports, particularly imports in governance and communication projects.

Recommendation 1.1: Promote transparency of AI imports and procurements.

Our study showed that public trust in AI and its use in the public domain is low, especially when Chinese donors and the local government do not provide adequate details on the deal package and the data source for the AI technology. We suggest that policymakers and NGOs in the recipient countries set up AI procurement policies to meet three key requirements: (1) best procurement standards, (2) implementation policies that meet high standards of protecting citizens, and (3) adequate availability to civil society of information on the outcomes and impacts of these projects. Potential lenders (such as the World Bank) and donors (including U.S. donors) can support recipient countries' governments to achieve the desired transparency. Encouraging recipient countries to follow the principle of transparency will foster trust, accountability, and responsible governance.

To achieve this, donors and recipient countries' governments and NGOs can promote open access data policies that allow citizens to access information related to aid use and project outcomes. By enhancing access to information, donors can empower local communities to actively participate in the development process and ensure that aid is used efficiently and effectively.

Additionally, donors should collaborate with recipient countries to establish robust monitoring and evaluation frameworks. These frameworks will enable donors to measure and communicate the impact of aid projects transparently, facilitating data-driven decisionmaking and continuous improvement.

Recommendation 1.2: Promote accountability by setting and following a national AI technology adoption strategy.

Such a strategy can aid in obtaining consensus on such issues as the rationale for importing AI, appropriate priority areas, and realistic expectations on AI-aided safe and smart cities. Developing countries often have many competing priorities and imperatives to address. Therefore, governments in recipient countries should prioritize discussions on the rationale for AI technology imports. The mass of Twitter users and interview subjects have many concerns and considerable skepticism about AI imports from other countries, whether from the United States or China. Many concerns focus on using AI in surveillance and military applications and whether a recipient country must rely on foreign technology and technical support for key national security domains. For example, if a nation imports AI without having the domestic talent that can maintain, upgrade, and adapt relevant systems, the country can become dependent on a foreign power for basic government needs, which is a dangerous proposition for any state that wants to remain independent. To build trust with the public, policymakers should permit the import of dual-use AI, such as surveillance systems, only with the strictest safeguards regarding their use. Military applications should be carefully partitioned from civilian use and kept under the monitoring of multipartisan entities and civil society.

It is also important to set realistic expectations concerning AI's ability to fight crime. As our interviewees argued, effective crime reduction should ultimately be rooted in finding and changing the social, structural, and economic causes of crime rather than relying solely on surveillance and policing to provide solutions. Widespread disappointment concerning the ability of expansive Safe City infrastructure to reduce crime underscores the need to conduct policy analysis to understand the limitations of AI technology.

Recommendation 2: Build country AI policies to manage data safety.

The adoption of new technologies in public service delivery, both by public agencies and private sector contractors, has created unprecedented levels of data on citizens' private lives. On the one hand, the availability of such timely datasets can enable improvements in service delivery models; on the other, these data can create serious security risks if they end up in the wrong hands. This situation is complicated by the fact that only a handful of countries have up-to-date data privacy laws and hardly any have operationalized them into a data governance system that would provide guidelines on the when, what, how, and why of intragovernment and public data-sharing.

If a new CCTV camera-based Smart City project collects real-time footage of police brutality, under which local laws and operational guidelines would law enforcement be entitled to share that footage with the media or in a court of law? The lack of clarity on such questions as this discourages local authorities from sharing data when its timely use could increase social welfare. To maximize the ethical, legal, and efficient use of publicly collected datasets, LMIC worldwide must develop their own customized data governance framework that contains clear guidelines on data-sharing, data privacy and protection, and data security protocols.

Recommendation 2.1: To minimize the potential harm of AI technology imports, a country's government should make sure that the country already has taken key steps before importing AI technology for use in the public sector.

The key steps that a country should take before importing AI technology use in the public sector include the following:

- Establish or strengthen data protection law and data governance structure.
- Support human capital development in trained AI professionals who understand AI technology well.
- Strengthen the political system, law enforcement, and regulatory capacities on AI technology.

Recommendation 2.2: Donors should conduct thorough assessments of existing data and AI policies within recipient countries.

These assessments will provide insights into the level of preparedness and maturity in handling data and technology. Furthermore, the assessments will help identify areas in which donor support is needed to strengthen policies and address potential risks. By offering targeted support to enhance data and AI policies, donors can ensure these technologies are harnessed responsibly, safeguarding individual rights and privacy while promoting innovation and progress.

Recommendation 3: Build local AI literacy and prepare to provide ancillary support for the AI application ecosystem.

The primary responsibility of ensuring that data protections are in place in the context of new projects lies with public officials in recipient countries. In many cases, because LMIC governance systems simply do not have the capacity to oversee complex data-intensive and legally complicated deployments, governments either end up overusing or underusing AI-enabling technology platforms.

Recommendation 3.1: Build local AI literacy.

Building local capacity is crucial for sustainable technological development and independence in developing countries. This involves educating the younger generation on AI, fostering local AI talent through education and training, supporting local tech entrepreneurship, and creating a conducive regulatory environment for innovation.

Recommendation 3.2: Provide ancillary support to the AI application ecosystem.

Our study found several advantages associated with China's AI exports: an integrated approach, affordability, flexibility, and data-driven insights. If other donors or investors are willing to compete in this field, they should consider providing such ancillary services.

This support should encompass various elements, including funding for capacity-building initiatives tailored to the specific needs of recipient countries. By empowering local communities and institutions with the skills and knowledge to leverage technology effectively, donors promote self-sufficiency and long-term impact.

Moreover, facilitating partnerships between local and international entities will promote knowledge exchange and enable the implementation of best practices. Auxiliary services, such as AI literacy programs, mentorship, market linkages, and infrastructure development, should also complement technology transfer to ensure its seamless integration into local settings.

In Closing: Geopolitical Competition Regarding AI and Its Consequences

The dawn of the AI era coincides with an era of geopolitical rivalry. AI is already a critical part of the U.S.-China competition. The technology decoupling between the United States and China is reshaping the global technological landscape, raising questions for the AI donor community and recipient countries. Should donors and recipients prepare for a two-world reality in which developing countries may have adopted technology infrastructures that are not fully compatible with the technology of the Western world? As we pointed out earlier, China's AI exports have advantages when competing with companies from other countries. However, some may argue that AI technology breakthroughs will be slower than expected with the U.S. sanctions on high-end chips and China's export restrictions on rare earth materials. Some might speculate that stricter regulations on AI in China will slow China's AI development compared with its main competitors.

The competition for dominating the AI sector may lead to interoperability issues if China and the United States develop their own protocols and standards. Supporting research and development efforts that bridge technological gaps and promote interoperability will help ensure that developing nations continue to benefit from technological advancements while staying connected with global trends.

The geopolitical and soft power competition might also mean that developing countries can attract more attention to development aid from large economies. Developing countries can leverage the market and open partnerships if the interoperability issues can be resolved.

Methodology for Building China's AI Exports Database (CAIED)

RAND researchers collaborated with AidData to create a first-of-its-kind interactive tool, showing China's AI influence in the developing world. The publications in this series are the first published studies to use quantitative and qualitative metrics to examine China's AI technology exports. The analysis summarized in this series reflects data available to the research team from AidData's GCDF 2.0, which covers the years 2000–2017. An updated GCDF 3.0 was made available in November 2023, and the research team is working on analyzing the new dataset, which extends the time horizon covered through 2021.

We built CAIED using version 2.0 of AidData's GCDF dataset.[1] To build CAIED, we screened for and extracted AI projects from the GCDF dataset, generated new AI application indicators (definitions can be found in Chapter 1), selected project-level variables, and added country governance and data policy variables. The project-level variables consisted of recipient country, project title, technology sector, project cost, project implementation status, project commitment year, project completion year, a short project description, project financial flow type, project financial concessionality, financial flow class, funding agencies, receiving agencies, and implementation agencies. These key variables offer a comprehensive overview of the individual AI projects contained in the dataset while also providing granular details, such as the implementation timeline and agencies involved in the project. The variables showcase financial and in-kind transfers from a wide variety of official donors and lenders, capture the terms and conditions of these financial flows, track the implementation of projects over time and geographic space, and include detailed narrative descriptions that explain how China's AI projects are being designed, implemented, monitored, and evaluated in practice.

The country governance variables in CAIED are rooted in two well-respected metrics of freedom and democracy indexes and two metrics of data protection policy status. One metric is the political regime metric (from 2022) based on results from the V-Dem democracy indexes in the Democracy Report produced by the V-Dem Institute.[2] The second metric, the electoral democracy index (from 2021), draws on the same source and represents an aggregate

---

[1] Custer et al., 2021; Dreher et al., 2022.

[2] Herre, Ortiz-Ospina, and Roser, 2013.

score based on freedom of association, clean elections, freedom of expression, elected officials, and suffrage.[3] The data protection metrics include the Data Protection Law Status variable from the United Nations Conference on Trade and Development, which tracks which countries have introduced or passed data protection.[4] Additionally, we replicate the scoring from the law firm DLA Piper, which grades every country's data protection level on a more detailed scale. A second metric from an independent source increases confidence in results, and the greater precision of the DLA Piper results might be useful for those who are less concerned about the risks of a potentially biased source, such as an independent law firm that conducts business in the countries in question.[5]

In the following sections, we explain the steps of constructing CAIED: (1) searching AI projects from the GCDF dataset, (2) generating new AI application indicators, (3) selecting project-level variables, and (4) adding additional country-level information. The description of the methodology presented in these sections is drawn from the companion report,[6] with minor adjustments.

Phase I: Developing String Lists for Searches

We conducted an initial review of the AidData GCDF 2.0 dataset, extracting the relevant strings identified during data collection activities. The initial string used for this preliminary scan was as follows: remote medicine, machine learning, algorithms, CCTV, Smart City, Safe City, surveillance. The preliminary scan returned a list of projects ($N = 70$), which the study team used to develop the test string list for the project search.

By reviewing and screening the project descriptions of the 70 projects, the study team extracted a list of strong keywords and a list of weak keywords (see Table A.1). The study team was also able to extract keywords specifically related to Chinese AI technology from the *China AI Development Report*.[7] Using these identified keywords, the study team conducted a further literature search on Google Scholar and extracted keywords relating to Chinese AI from multiple recently published studies.[8] Finally, the study team consulted more than ten

---

[3] Herre, Ortiz-Ospina, and Roser, 2013.

[4] United Nations Conference on Trade and Development, 2021.

[5] DLA Piper, undated.

[6] Bouey et al., 2023b.

[7] China Institute for Science and Technology Policy at Tsinghua University, *China AI Development Report*, 2018.

[8] Amazon Web Services, "What Is Deep Learning?" webpage, undated; Santosh Gaikwad, Bharti W. Gawali, and Pravin Yannawar, "A Review on Speech Recognition Technique," *International Journal of Computer Applications*, Vol. 10, No. 3, 2010; Carson K. Leung, Peter Braun, and Alfredo Cuzzocrea, "AI-Based Sensor Information Fusion for Supporting Deep Supervised Learning" *Sensors*, Vol. 19, No. 6, 2019; Praksh M. Nadkarni, Lucila Ohno-Machado, and Wendy W. Chapman, "Natural Language Processing: An Intro-

TABLE A.1

Summary of Keywords from Literature Review

Source	Strong Keywords	Weak Keywords
Keywords extracted from preliminary scan	intelligent applications	surveillance, CCTV
		video surveillance
	intelligent video surveillance	information system
		security surveillance network
		video monitoring system, software
		video surveillance
		Safe City, big data
		smart camera
	intelligent alert system	remote monitoring
Keywords extracted from the *China AI Development Report*	speech recognition, speech synthesis, voiceprint recognition, human-machine dialogue	speech recognition, speech synthesis, speech interaction, speech evaluation, human-machine dialogue, voiceprint recognition
	facial recognition, visual recognition, affective computing, expression recognition, behavior recognition, gesture recognition, body recognition, mobile vision, OCR, handwriting recognition, text recognition, image processing, image recognition, pattern recognition, spatial recognition	biometrics (face recognition, iris recognition, fingerprint recognition, vein recognition, etc.), affective computing, emotion recognition, expression recognition, behavior recognition, gesture recognition, body recognition, video content recognition, object and scene recognition, mobile vision, optical character recognition (OCR), handwriting recognition, text recognition, image processing, image recognition, pattern recognition, SLAM, spatial recognition, 3D scanning, 3D reconstruction, etc.
	natural language processing	natural language interaction, natural language understanding, semantic understanding, machine translation, text mining (semantic analysis, semantic computing, classification, clustering), information extraction, human-machine interaction
	basic algorithm and platform	machine learning, deep learning, open source framework, open platform
	basic hardware (semiconductor, GPU)	chips, lidars, sensors, etc.
	basic enabling technology	cloud computing, big data
	intelligent robotics (including solutions)	industrial robotics, service robotics, personal/home robotics, home security robot, in-vehicle robot
	smart driving (including solutions)	intelligent driving, driverless driving, autonomous driving, assisted driving, advanced driver assistance system (ADAS), laser radar, ultrasonic radar, millimeter wave radar, GPS positioning, high-precision map, vehicle chip, human-car interaction

Table A.1—Continued

Source	Strong Keywords	Weak Keywords
	drone (including solutions)	consumer drones, professional drones
	AI+	finance, insurance, judiciary administration, entertainment, tourism, healthcare, education, logistics and warehousing, smart home, smart city, network security, video surveillance, commerce, human resources, corporate services
Keywords extracted from literature review	speech recognition	speech processing, signal processing, pattern recognition
	face recognition	face recognition, face perception, facial recognition techniques
	affective computing	smart surveillance, perceptual interface, human-computer interaction, emotional speech processing, prosody
	pattern recognition	
	text recognition	unsupervised, feature learning, text detection, character recognition, text recognition, pretraining
	natural language	natural language, NLP, lexer
	deep learning	convolutional nets, recurrent nets, deep learning, image processing, video processing, linear classifier, multilayer architectures, backpropogation
	sensors	sensor information fusion, supervised learning, data mining
		expert systems, fuzzy systems, natural language processing, speech recognition, pattern recognition, computer vision, decision-support systems, knowledge bases, neural networks
	intelligent robotics	smart technology, artificial intelligence, robotics, and algorithms (STARA)
		general artificial intelligence, narrow artificial intelligence
		AI robotics
	smart driving artificial intelligence	internet of things (IoT), physical internet (PI), industry 4.0
		blockchain-AI, intelligent transportation systems, intelligence transport system
	drone artificial intelligence	drones, object detection, feature extraction, detectors, classifier, deep learning, detection, image processing
		drone network, drone communication, drone communication security

Table A.1—Continued

Source	Strong Keywords	Weak Keywords
	AI+ artificial intelligence	radiology, computed tomography, Image analysis
	China AI development mechanisms	representation learning, deep learning, supervised learning, unsupervised learning
		healthcare AI applications, AI-based screening and referral system
		Arterys, IDx-DR, Guardian Connect (Medtronic)
		Chinese language information processing
		new concept weapons, cyber warfare
		automation in manufacturing, digital environmental protection, social credit system
		internet plus
		computer vision, natural language processing, trans-media analysis and reasoning, intelligent adaptive learning, collective intelligence, automated unmanned systems, intelligent chips, brain-computer interfaces
		unmanned aerial vehicles (UAVs), voice and image recognition

Additional Keywords
NLU, natural language generation (NLG), autonomous vehicles, self-driving cars, chatbot(s), large language models (LLMs), training data, test data, validation data, data science, modelling, augmented reality, long short-term memory (LSTM), support vector machine (SVM), t-distributed stochastic neighbor embedding (TSNE), automated reasoning, ensemble methods, feature learning, feature selection, generative adversarial network, machine perception, Monte Carlo, swarm AI/swarm intelligence, entity recognition/named-entity recognition (NER), dimensionality reduction, principal component analysis (PCA), python, reinforcement learning (RL), dataframe(s), Turing, big data, recommendation system, data mining, page rank, search engine, anomaly detection, sentiment analysis, graph optimization

NOTE: AI+ = AI + human intelligence; GPU = graphics processing unit; NLP = natural language processing; NLU = natural language understanding; SLAM = simultaneous localization and mapping.

researchers and professionals working in the technology industry to suggest additional keywords that might help us identify AI projects from the AidData GCDF 2.0 Dataset.

The study team ran an initial search within AidData's GCDF 2.0 Dataset using all of the keywords and extracted strings with positive matches. These strings were combined into

duction," *Journal of the American Medical Informatics Association*, Vol. 18, No. 5, 2011; Jianhua Tao and Tieniu Tan, "Affective Computing: A Review," *Affective Computing and Intelligent Interaction: First International Conference, ACII 2005, Beijing, October 22–24, 2005, Proceedings*, Springer, October 2005; Daniel Zhang, Saurabh Mishra, Erik Brynjolfsson, John Etchemendy, Deep Ganguli, Barbara Grosz, Terah Lyons, James Manyika, Juan Carlos Niebles, Michael Sellitto, Yoav Shoham, Jack Clark, and Raymond Perrault, *The AI Index 2021 Annual Report*, AI Index Steering Committee, Human-Centered AI Institute, Stanford University, March 2021; Tao Wang, David J. Wu, Adam Coates, and Andrew Y. Ng, "End-to-End Text Recognition with Convolutional Neural Networks," *Proceedings of the 21st International Conference on Pattern Recognition (ICPR2012)*, 2012; Zhao et al., 2003; W. Zhao, R. Chellappa, P. J. Phillips, and A. Rosenfeld, "Face Recognition: A Literature Survey," *ACM Computing Surveys (CSUR)*, Vol. 35, No. 4, December 2003.

a test string list for the test run: CCTV, smart city, safe city, surveillance, facial recognition, machine learning, image, e-governance, data, remote, algorithm, video, consultation, AI (Artificial Intelligence), recognition, ICT (information and communication technology), information system, network, monitoring, software, camera, OCR (optical character recognition), scanning, computing, digital, drone, 3D, natural language, chip, sensor, semiconductor, robot, laser, radar, network security, urban security, information technology, IoT (Internet of Things), blockchain, object detection, automation, unmanned, UAV (unmanned aerial vehicle), augmented reality.

To address case sensitivity in string detection, we employed a function to convert all project description text to lowercase during the string detection process. The initial results from the test run reported 2,412 projects, with only 30 strings returning valid output: CCTV, smart city, safe city, surveillance, image, data, remote, algorithm, video, consultation, recognition, ICT, information system, monitoring, software, camera, OCR, scanning, computing, digital, 3D, chip, sensor, robot, laser, network security, information technology, IoT, automation, UAV.

After summarizing the statistics from the frequency table of the strings, we identified two issues related to false positive results. The first issue is nonexact matches triggering false positives for many strings. During the analysis of the strings used in the test run, it was observed that nonexact matches were causing false positives for several strings. Examples of these false positives include following: The string "iot" returned matches such as "antibiotics," "riots," and "physiotherapy" instead of the intended meaning; the string "ict" returned matches such as "victims," "district," and "conflict" instead of the intended meaning; the string "data" returned matches such as "AidData" and "Chinese Loans to Africa Database" instead of the intended meaning.

To address this issue, we implemented a solution by creating a new section in the string processing script. This new section was designed to distinguish between strings for vague matches and strings for strict matches. For the strict matches, the team added "\\b" as boundaries for the strings, enabling strict matching. The vague match strings list includes strings such as "surveillance," "automation," "robot," "recognition," "e-governance," and "facial recognition." On the other hand, all other strings were set to strict match and constructed with boundaries in the script.

The second issue identified is that certain strings in the initial list were too broad in their scope. To address this issue, the study team reviewed and refined the strings and narrowed their focus. The refined string list that emerged from this collaboration is as follows: CCTV, smart city, safe city, surveillance, facial recognition, machine learning, image, e-governance, data center, government data, remote, algorithm, video, consultation, AI, artificial intelligence, recognition, ICT, information system, neural network, monitoring, software, camera, OCR, scanning, computing, digital environmental protection, drone, 3D, natural language, chip, sensor, semiconductor, robot, laser, radar, network security, urban security, information technology, IoT, blockchain, object detection, automation, unmanned, UAV, augmented reality, CT (Computed Tomography), PET (Positron Emission Tomography), MRI (Magnetic Resonance Imaging), ultrasound.

These refined strings provide a more targeted and specific representation of the concepts and technologies related to the analysis of Chinese development finance projects.

Phase II: Adjusting String Lists and Conducting Manual Reviews

Test runs were performed using the new string detection script and modified string list. We further enhanced the analysis by merging AidData's military projects and Huawei projects with the Chinese development finance projects. The combined dataset was used for a second round of string detection. In this round, 697 projects were analyzed, and 36 strings returned valid output. To ensure the accuracy of the results, the study team established a manual review workflow for thorough screening of the project outcomes.

Following a meticulous manual review of the 697 projects and excluding those that were clearly not related to AI (false positives), the final result revealed 81 projects categorized as "yes" (confirmed AI application) and 101 projects classified as "maybe" (potential AI application). The 81 "yes" projects were projects that clearly used AI technologies, such as speech recognition, facial recognition, NLP, deep learning, intelligent robotics, and drones. We also consulted experts with specialty in AI to confirm that the "yes" projects used AI technology (see the next section for details). The 101 "maybe" projects were projects that can possibly include AI technology, but the specific technology was not explicitly mentioned in the project description.

Phase III: Refining Search Keywords and Conducting Recovery Search

To make sure that our string list is comprehensive, we consulted researchers who have expertise in AI technology applications in four sectors to which most of the "yes" (confirmed AI application) projects belong: communication, government and civil society, health, and education. We specifically asked about the experts' suggestions on the comprehensiveness of the string list. We also sought their opinions on how to code the "maybe" projects by providing them with the project descriptions and the potential AI application technologies.

From experts' responses, we were able to collect the additional search keywords:

- general AI keywords: cat scanner, broadband, fiber optic, biometric, smart
- communication sector AI keywords: 4G, 5G, 6G, radio, transceiver, training (chips), Global System for Mobile communication, CDMA, crypto, Coalition for Content and
- Provenance and Authenticity (C2PA), computational thinking, digitization

- education-sector AI keywords: intelligent tutoring, language models, education technology, automated essay scoring, latent semantic analysis
- health-sector AI keywords: diagnosis, quality improvement, health information technology (HIT), electronic health record (EHR), electronic medical record (EMR), clinical decision support (CDS, or sometimes CDSS for clinical decision support systems), digital health, smart devices, medical device, digital medicine, eHealth and variants (e-Health, etc.)
- government-sector AI keywords: disaster, disaster risk reduction, community resilience, Sendai framework, preparedness, mitigation, response, recovery, UN Disaster Risk Reduction (UNDRR), humanitarian action, triple nexus, Grand Bargain.

Our study team screened the additional keywords and created the following string list to conduct a recovery project search: 5G, 6G, CDMA, broadband, digitization, computational thinking, C2PA, biometric, crypto, e-health, eHealth, digital medicine, smart devices, health information technology, electronic health record, digital health, generative, automated, intelligent tutoring, clinical decision support, CAT scan.

We then screened all the projects from this recovery search and filtered out 51 additional "maybe" (potential AI application) projects.

Phase IV: Generating the AI Application Indicator

Refining Coding Criteria and Rules

Since there is no universal rule in defining AI technology, we generated an indicator to differentiate between two AI project categories. One category contains *AI application* projects that directly use AI technologies, such as facial recognition, speech recognition, and algorithms that facilitate medical diagnosis. The other contains *AI infrastructure* projects, such as building data centers, connecting 5G network technology, laying fiber optical cables, training in AI technology, and installing AI hardware (such as CCTV cameras) that provide the necessary platform for AI deployment.

Using the suggestions and feedback from the experts we consulted, we were able to develop a set of rules for coding the "maybe" projects into AI application projects or AI infrastructure projects. The study team also paid special attention to the implementing agencies or companies and the implementation year to determine whether a project might have any AI components.

AI Rating Scales (Levels 1–5)

1. something for which AI impossible or irrelevant
2. something that could have AI applied to it (e.g., broadband)
3. something that is AI-empowered or -powered, but most of the value is not AI (e.g., X-ray scanners)

4. something explicitly for AI use (e.g., CCTV for smart cities)
5. data center for AI.

Coding Rules on the AI Application Indicator

- We excluded **level 1** projects that belong to the following categories:
  - e-government projects that implement only documentational management systems
  - projects that involve only training of human capital (not specifically mentioning AI content in training)
  - medical devices and technologies that have no AI components (all the health projects except the ones identified above in the "yes" and AI infrastructure categories)
  - disease surveillance projects in the database that were implemented quite early and were designed for specific countries
  - generalized equipment, such as equipment for a mining project or a hospital, without additional detail
  - projects that are mostly non-AI, such as an electricity grid, oil rigs, or a hospital building (even if the project has a small AI software component) and are not implemented by a Chinese AI company[9]
  - CDMA or radio station projects that do not mention any AI component.
- We coded **level 2** and **level 3** projects that belong to the following categories as AI infrastructure projects:
  - projects that involve the building of data centers
  - CDMA or radio station projects that were implemented after 2012 and specifically mention any AI components
  - communication projects that installed any fiber optics, signal towers, satellites, or other supporting infrastructure for AI
  - e-government projects that built electrical management systems with AI technology
  - projects that installed CCTV cameras for detection and recognition purposes
  - projects on human capital training programs that especially involve AI technology or were implemented by a Chinese AI company
  - projects that involve container scanners manufactured by a Chinese AI company
  - seismic monitoring projects that collect data that have a very high likelihood of being processed by machine learning models
  - medical imaging projects that could theoretically involve AI technologies.
- We coded **level 4** and **level 5** projects that belong to the following categories as AI application projects:
  - projects that substantially involve biometric identity detection, anti–electricity theft, or anomaly detection technologies
  - health projects that substantially involve automated radiology

---

[9] We gathered a list of Chinese AI companies from multiple sources, including various research institutions' reports and articles, AI company rankings on private company websites, and AI expert consultations.

    – safe and/or smart city projects that either substantially involve surveillance cameras or were implemented by a Chinese AI company.

Coding the "Maybe" Projects from the Manual Review

According to these rules that we developed and refined, three analysts of the team individually coded the 101 "maybe" projects using the AI application indicator. The codes from the three analysts are the same for 81 "maybe" projects. For the remaining 20 "maybe" projects that involve discrepancies in the codes, the analysts compared and discussed the code and used the majority result as the final code (e.g., if two analysts code a project as an AI application project and one analyst codes it as an AI infrastructure project, the final AI application indicator for this project will be AI project).

Coding the "Maybe" Projects from the Recovery Search

In addition, the study team followed the same steps to code the AI applications indicator for the 51 "maybe" projects screened out from the recovery search. All of the 51 projects fall under the exclusion criteria.

This manual review process allowed us to exclude a total of 549 projects from the 697 projects that returned from the adjusted search. We selected 94 AI application projects and 54 AI infrastructure projects to include in the CAIED.

Salvaging Projects That Were Originally Excluded

To ensure that the original manual coding that we conducted also followed the same rule, the study team conducted another manual review of all the 549 projects that were excluded from the original manual review. We found seven projects that were recorded as AI infrastructure projects according to the refined coding criteria and rules we created. Four of these AI infrastructure projects are surveillance projects that involved installations of cameras. The other three projects belong to e-government, medical imaging, and security scanners. These seven AI infrastructure projects were incorporated into the CAIED.

Finalizing the Selection of AI Application and AI Infrastructure Projects

Lastly, the study team conducted a manual review of any potential duplicate projects to confirm that projects with similar purposes and sectors were, indeed, separate financial transactions. In the final CAIED, we include 94 AI application projects and 61 AI infrastructure projects (54 from manually coding the "maybe" projects and seven from salvaging the excluded projects).

Phase V: Selecting Variables from the AidData GCDF 2.0 Dataset

The AidData team and RAND jointly selected a subset of 15 key variables from the broader AidData GCDF 2.0 dataset. This includes **Recipient Country, Title, AidData Project ID, Sector, Amount, Implementation Status, Commitment Year, Completion Year, Description, Flow Type, Concessionality, Flow Class, Funding Agencies, Receiving Agencies**, and **Implementation Agencies**. We shortened the AidData project titles for concision. These key variables offer a comprehensive overview of the individual AI projects included in the dataset while also providing granular details, such as the implementation timeline and agencies involved in the project. The variables showcase financial and in-kind transfers from a wide range of official donors and lenders; capture the terms and conditions of these financial flows; track the implementation of projects over time and geographic space; and include detailed narrative descriptions that explain how China's AI projects are being designed, implemented, monitored, and evaluated in practice. Reporting specifics on the financial flow amount, type, class, and sector, consistent with OECD-DAC reporting directives, allows users the opportunity to compare China's financing with other sources of development finance, including members of the OECD-DAC and multilateral institutions.

Phase VI: Adding in Technology Categories and Country-Level Information

To help users better understand the content of the projects at a glance, we created the technology category variable using the information from the detailed project description. The technology category variable includes the eight most commonly used general AI technology types of Chinese AI exports in the dataset, including Advanced Computing and Data Storage, e-Government, Medical Imaging, Remote Sensing and Seismic Monitor, Safe and Smart City, Security Scanners, Unmanned Vehicles, and Other. The Other category includes educational AI-training projects.

In addition, we created an indicator showing the purpose of AI technology usage using the information from the detailed project description and flow class provided in the AidData GCDF 2.0 dataset. The usage variable currently has two categories, Military and Civilian.

To provide users with context, we added several columns from outside AidData. We included three metrics of freedom and democracy and two metrics of data protection.

Because of the perceptions of China and the impact of AI-powered surveillance, we included three metrics of the political state of the country. The first was the **political regime** (of the year 2022), drawing from Our World in Data, which, in turn, relied on results from the Varieties of Democracy (V-Dem) Institute democracy indices in the *Democracy Report*

2022.[10] The well-respected V-Dem indices are developed by political scientists and funded by the World Bank and several governments: V-Dem is a credible and independent source. The second, the **Electoral Democracy Index** (of the year 2021), draws on the same source and represents an aggregate score based on freedom of association, clean elections, freedom of expression, elected officials, and suffrage. The third was the **Freedom House rating**, "the most widely read and cited report of its kind": It is less precise but more popular and so was also included.[11]

The United Nations Conference on Trade and Development keeps track of which countries have introduced or passed data protection laws—Data Protection Metrics. These were incorporated in our **Data Protection Law Status** column.[12] Additionally, the law firm DLA Piper grades every country's data protection level on a more detailed scale. We replicate that scoring here. A second metric from an independent source, DLA Piper's mapping of the levels of global data protection laws, increases confidence in results, and the greater precision of the DLA Piper results may be useful for those who are less concerned about the risks of a potentially biased source, such as an independent law firm with business in the countries in question.[13]

All data acquired from the external data sources listed above were last accessed as of April 28, 2023.

---

[10] Herre, Ortiz-Ospina, and Roser, 2013; V-Dem Institute, *Democracy Report 2022: Autocratization Changing Nature?* March 2022.

[11] Freedom House, undated-b.

[12] United Nations Conference on Trade and Development, 2021.

[13] DLA Piper, 2023.

Methodology for the Qualitative Interviews and Social Media Analysis

In-Depth Stakeholder Interviews

We used a qualitative research methodology, conducting in-depth interviews with a practical purposive sample of stakeholders with expertise in AI technology from civil society, the business sector, government, and academia. We identified the initial interviewees within the study team's professional networks and used the snowball sampling method by asking for introductions to stakeholders who would be most suitable for the interviews. The stakeholders were invited to participate in the study through their email or through the organizations' publicly accessible email addresses.

We designed and developed an interview protocol that contained 20 questions regarding the interviewee's background and involvement in AI projects, the purpose and applications of AI technology, AI project implementers, and data security and risks related to AI technology. Using this interview protocol as the interview guideline, we conducted semistructured interviews in English until we reached data saturation. A total of 18 interviews were conducted: eight in Pakistan and ten in Kenya.

We developed the codebook based on the interview protocol and then read and coded the 18 interview transcripts using an axial coding approach. We then discussed and identified the prominent emerging themes and patterns from the coded interview excerpts.

Social Media Analysis Data Collection

Twitter data were collected via Brandwatch. To find tweets that mentioned the United States, we used ("USA" OR "America"); to find tweets that mentioned China, we used ("China" OR "Chinese"). To find tweets that mentioned AI, we used a more complicated search, drawing on an iterative refinement procedure for determining search terms described in greater detail in the companion report,[1] as follows:

> "cctv" OR "smart city" OR "safe city" OR "surveil" OR "facial rec*" OR "machine learning" OR "image" OR "e-govern" OR "data" OR "remote" OR "algorithm" OR "video" OR "consultation" OR "ai" OR "artificial intelligence" OR "recognition" OR "ict" OR "information system" OR "network" OR "monitor" OR "software" OR "camera" OR "ocr" OR "scan" OR "computing" OR "digital" OR "drone" OR "natural language" OR "chip" OR "sensor" OR "semiconductor" OR "robot" OR "laser" OR "radar" OR "network security" OR "urban security" OR "information technology" OR "iot" OR "blockchain" OR "object detection" OR "automat" OR "unmanned" OR "uav" OR "augmented reality"

---

[1]   Bouey et al., 2023b.

Abbreviations

AI	artificial intelligence
BRI	Belt and Road Initiative
CAIED	China's AI Exports Database
CCTV	closed-circuit television
CDMA	code-division multiple access
CPEC	China-Pakistan Economic Corridor
DAC	Development Assistance Committee
GCDF	Global Chinese Development Finance
ICT	information and communication technology
LMIC	low- and middle-income countries
NADRA	National Database and Registration Authority
NGO	nongovernmental organization
OECD	Organisation for Economic Co-operation and Development
UAV	unmanned aerial vehicle

References

Abdullah, "Transsion: Q2 Brings Strong Growth for Africa's Leading Phone Seller," *Gizchina*, July 30, 2023.

Afzal, Madiha, *"At All Costs": How Pakistan and China Control the Narrative on the China-Pakistan Economic Corridor*, Brookings Institution, June 2020.

Ahmed, Zaboor, Khurram Khaliq Bhinder, Amna Tariq, Muhammad Junaid Tahir, Qasim Mehmood, Muhammad Saad Tabassum, Muna Malik, Sana Aslam, Muhammad Sohaib Asghar, and Zohaib Yousaf, "Knowledge, Attitude, and Practice of Artificial Intelligence Among Doctors and Medical Students in Pakistan: A Cross-Sectional Online Survey," *Annals of Medicine and Surgery*, Vol. 76, 2022.

AidData, "Global Chinese Development Finance," webpage, undated. As of November 21, 2023: https://china.aiddata.org

AidData, AidData's Global Chinese Development Finance Dataset, version 2.0, database, September 29, 2021. As of November 1, 2023: https://www.aiddata.org/data/aiddatas-global-chinese-development-finance-dataset-version-2-0

Amazon Web Services, "What Is Deep Learning?" webpage, undated. As of October 27, 2023: https://aws.amazon.com/what-is/deep-learning

Barboza, David, and John Markoff, "Power in Numbers: China Aims for High-Tech Primacy," *New York Times*, December 5, 2011.

Beraja, Martin, Andrew Kao, David Y. Yang, and Noam Yuchtman, *Exporting the Surveillance State via Trade in AI*, Brookings Institution, January 2023.

Bhutta, Zafar, "Govt to Use NADRA's Database to Detect Tax Evaders," *Express Tribune*, March 13, 2019.

Bouey, Jennifer, Lynn Hu, Keller Scholl, William Marcellino, Stacey Yi, Rafiq Dossani, James Gazis, Ammar A. Malik, Kyra Solomon, Sheng Zhang, and Andy Shufer, *China's AI Exports Database (CAIED)*, RAND Corporation, TL-A2696-1, 2023a. As of December 11, 2023: https://www.rand.org/pubs/tools/TLA2696-1.html

Bouey, Jennifer, Lynn Hu, Keller Scholl, William Marcellino, James Gazis, Ammar A. Malik, Kyra Solomon, Sheng Zhang, and Andy Shufer, *China's AI Exports: Developing a Tool to Track Chinese Development Finance in the Global South—Technical Documentation*, RAND Corporation, RR-A2696-1, 2023b. As of December 11, 2023: https://www.rand.org/pubs/research_reports/RRA2696-1.html

China Institute for Science and Technology Policy at Tsinghua University, *China AI Development Report*, 2018.

Chutel, Lynsey, "China Is Exporting Facial Recognition Software to Africa, Expanding Its Vast Database," *Quartz*, May 25, 2018.

Custer, Samantha, Axel Dreher, Thai-Binh Elston, Andreas Fuchs, Siddharta Ghose, Joyce Jiahul Lin, Ammar A. Malik, Bradley C. Parks, Brooke Russell, Kyra Solomon, Austin Strange, Michael J. Tierney, Katherine Walsh, Lincoln Zaleski, and Sheng Zhang, *Tracking Chinese Development Finance: An Application of AidData's TUFF 2.0 Methodology*, AidData at William & Mary, September 29, 2021.

Devex, "National Database and Registration Authority (NADRA)," webpage, undated. As of October 31, 2023:
https://www.devex.com/organizations/national-database-and-registration-authority-nadra-25293

Ding, Jeffrey, "China's Current Capabilities, Policies, and Industrial Ecosystem in AI," testimony before the U.S.-China Economic and Security Review Commission Hearing on Technology, Trade, and Military-Civil Fusion: China's Pursuit of Artificial Intelligence, New Materials, and New Energy, June 7, 2019.

DLA Piper, Data Protection Laws of the World, database, undated. As of October 30, 2023:
https://www.dlapiperdataprotection.com

DLA Piper, "Kenya," webpage, last updated January 12, 2023. As of October 30, 2023:
https://www.dlapiperdataprotection.com/index.html?c2=&c=KE&t=law

Dreher, Axel, Andreas Fuchs, Bradley Parks, Austin Strange, and Michael J. Tierney, *Banking on Beijing: The Aims and Impacts of China's Overseas Development Program*, Cambridge University Press, 2022.

Ekwealor, Victor, "In Africa, OPay and WeChat Have More in Common Than Just Being Super Apps," Techpoint Africa, November 29, 2019.

Fazl-E-Haider, Syed, "China's Big Gamble in Pakistan: A 10-Year Scorecard for CPEC," *The Interpreter*, August 1, 2023.

Freedom House, "Country and Territory Ratings and Statuses, 1973–2023," spreadsheet, undated-a.

Freedom House, "Freedom in the World," webpage, undated-b. As of October 30, 2023:
https://freedomhouse.org/report/freedom-world

Gaikwad, Santosh K., Bharti W. Gawali, and Pravin Yannawar, "A Review on Speech Recognition Technique," *International Journal of Computer Applications*, Vol. 10, No. 3, 2010.

Graham, Brad, and Caleb Stroup, "Does Anti-Bribery Enforcement Deter Foreign Investment?" *Applied Economics Letters*, Vol. 23, No. 1, 2016.

Herre, Bastian, "The 'Regimes of the World' Data: How Do Researchers Measure Democracy?" webpage, Our World in Data, December 2, 2021. As of October 30, 2023:
https://ourworldindata.org/regimes-of-the-world-data

Herre, Bastian, Esteban Ortiz-Ospina, and Max Roser, "Democracy," webpage, Our World in Data, 2013. As of October 30, 2023:
https://ourworldindata.org/democracy

Hersey, Frank, "NGOs Sue Idemia for Failing to Consider Human Rights Risks in Kenyan Digital ID," Biometric Update, July 29, 2022.

Human Rights Watch, "Pakistan: Mass Arrests Target Political Opposition," May 20, 2023.

Jamal, Sana, "Pakistan, China Urged to Boost Tech Cooperation," *Gulf News*, July 20, 2022.

Jili, Bulelani, "Chinese Surveillance Tools in Africa," China, Law, and Development Project, University of Oxford, 2020.

Jili, Bulelani, "Africa's Demand for and Adoption of Chinese Surveillance Technology," Atlantic Council's Digital Forensic Research Lab, May 2023.

Leung, Carson K., Peter Braun, and Alfredo Cuzzocrea, "AI-Based Sensor Information Fusion for Supporting Deep Supervised Learning," *Sensors*, Vol. 19, No. 6, 2019.

Luong, Ngor, and Zachary Arnold, *China's Artificial Intelligence Industry Alliance: Understanding China's AI Strategy Through Industry Alliances*, Center for Security and Emerging Technology, May 2021.

Mai, Jun, "Technology Key to China's Vision for the Future as a World Leading Power," *South China Morning Post*, March 6, 2021.

Malik, Ammar A., Bradley Parks, Brooke Russell, Joyce Jiahui Lin, Katherine Walsh, Kyra Solomon, Sheng Zhang, Thai-Binh Elston, and Seth Goodman, *Banking on the Belt and Road: Insights from a New Global Dataset of 13,427 Chinese Development Projects*, AidData at William & Mary, September 29, 2021.

Mandon, Pierre, and Martha Tesfaye Woldemichael, "Has Chinese Aid Benefitted Recipient Countries?" Brookings Institution, April 6, 2023.

March, Jenni, "How China Is Slowly Expanding Its Power in Africa, One TV Set at a Time," CNN, July 24, 2019.

Miller, Manjari Chatterjee, "How China and Pakistan Forged Close Ties," Council on Foreign Relations, October 3, 2022.

Montgomery, Mark, and Eric Sayers, "Don't Let China Take over the Cloud—US National Security Depends on It," *The Hill*, November 13, 2023.

Mureithi, Muriuki, and Judy Nyaguthii, *Telecommunication Ecosystem Evolution in Kenya 2009–2019: Setting the Pace and Unbundling the Turbulent Journey to a Digital Economy in a 4IR Era*, Institute of Economic Affairs, 2021.

Murthy, Dhiraj, Alexander Gross, and Alexander Pensavalle, "Urban Social Media Demographics: An Exploration of Twitter Use in Major American Cities," *Journal of Computer-Mediated Communication*, Vol. 21, No. 1, January 1, 2016.

OECD—*See* Organisation for Economic Co-operation and Development.

Organisation for Economic Co-operation and Development, "DAC and CRS Code Lists," webpage, undated. As of October 30, 2023:
https://www.oecd.org/dac/financing-sustainable-development/development-finance-standards/dacandcrscodelists.htm

Nadkarni, Prakash M., Lucila Ohno-Machado, and Wendy W. Chapman, "Natural Language Processing: An Introduction," *Journal of the American Medical Informatics Association*, Vol. 18, No. 5, 2011.

Pakistani.org, "Part II: Fundamental Rights and Principles of Policy," The Constitution of the Islamic Republic of Pakistan, webpage, undated. As of October 30, 2023:
https://www.pakistani.org/pakistan/constitution/part2.ch1.html

Punjab Safe Cities Authority, *Data and Privacy Protection Procedures (DP3)*, undated.

Sheehan, Matt, *China's AI Regulations and How They Get Made*, Carnegie Endowment for International Peace, July 10, 2023.

Silver, Laura, Christine Huang, and Laura Clancy, "China's Approach to Foreign Policy Gets Largely Negative Reviews in 24-Country Survey," Pew Research Center, July 27, 2023.

Tao, Jianhua, and Tieniu Tan, "Affective Computing: A Review," *Affective Computing and Intelligent Interaction: First International Conference, ACII 2005, Beijing, October 22–24, 2005, Proceedings*, Springer, October 2005.

United Nations Conference on Trade and Development, Data Protection and Privacy Legislation Worldwide, database, December 14, 2021. As of October 30, 2023:
https://unctad.org/page/data-protection-and-privacy-legislation-worldwide

V-Dem Institute, *Democracy Report 2022: Autocratization Changing Nature?* March 2022. As of November 20, 2023:
https://v-dem.net/media/publications/dr_2022.pdf

Wang, Tao, David J. Wu, Adam Coates, and Andrew Y. Ng, "End-to-End Text Recognition with Convolutional Neural Networks," *Proceedings of the 21st International Conference on Pattern Recognition (ICPR2012)*, 2012.

Webster, Graham, Rogier Creemers, Elsa Kania, and Paul Triolo, "Full Translation: China's 'New Generation Artificial Intelligence Development Plan' (2017)," webpage, DigiChina, August 1, 2017. As of October 30, 2023:
https://digichina.stanford.edu/work/full-translation-chinas-new-generation-artificial-intelligence-development-plan-2017

Zhang, Daniel, Saurabh Mishra, Erik Brynjolfsson, John Etchemendy, Deep Ganguli, Barbara Grosz, Terah Lyons, James Manyika, Juan Carlos Niebles, Michael Sellitto, Yoav Shoham, Jack Clark, and Raymond Perrault, *The AI Index 2021 Annual Report*, AI Index Steering Committee, Human-Centered AI Institute, Stanford University, March 2021.

Zhao, W., R. Chellappa, P. J. Phillips, and A. Rosenfeld, "Face Recognition: A Literature Survey," *ACM Computing Surveys (CSUR)*, Vol. 35, No. 4, December 2003.